# IN HIS PATHWAY

# IN HIS PATHWAY

## The Story of
## REV WILLIAM McCREA

*As told to*

DAVID PORTER

MARSHALL MORGAN & SCOTT

Lakeland
Marshall, Morgan & Scott
*a Pentos company*
1 Bath Street, London EC1V 9LB


First published 1980 by Marshall Morgan & Scott

ISBN 0 551 00893 8



Impression number: 10 9 8 7 6 5 4 3 2 1

Photoset in Great Britain by
Rowland Phototypesetting Ltd
Bury St Edmunds, Suffolk
Printed in Great Britain by
Hunt Barnard Printing Ltd., Aylesbury

This book is dedicated to
my wife and family

The statements made in this book are true to the best of my knowledge, and the opinions expressed are honestly held.

*William McCrea*

He gave his life for me,
His precious blood he shed;
A crown of thorns he wore,
Upon his head.

Why didst thou, Lord,
Have wondrous love for me?
Lord, at thy feet I cast
My life to thee.

Take all I am – or, even,
Hope, Lord to be –
Until at last
We reign eternally . . .

*William McCrea*

# Contents

# Introduction

David Porter

Belfast and its surrounding countryside, spread out like a pocket handkerchief, stood alarmingly on edge as the plane banked sharply and began its descent into Aldergrove Airport. For a moment the whole Province seemed to hang, green and vertical, like a map on the wall. Then we were landing in the airport, and I emerged into a sharp clear Ulster morning. It was my first visit to Northern Ireland.

The Rev William McCrea arrived in his car. He was apologetic. 'I've got a busy day,' he said. 'We'll have to talk in between.' He is a slightly built man, and most of his actions are quick and decisive. The later pictures on his album sleeves are pretty good portraits; if he ever was the diffident youth that looks out from the covers of his early albums, he has certainly changed. William McCrea knows where he is going.

We headed for Belfast, joining the broad M2 motorway, and arrived shortly at the Royal Victoria Hospital, Belfast, where one of his congregation was recovering in the Intensive Care Unit and had asked to see him. While he was in the Hospital, I sat in the car, but it was only a short visit and we were soon driving back into the city centre. William was due at a meeting of a Common Market committee at 11 am (where he planned to argue against the EEC). He chatted to Local Government colleagues in the splendid marbled entrance lobby of the Belfast City Hall where the meeting was to take place, having first secured the ear of a friendly attendant who sat me down with a cup of coffee in a comfortable anteroom.

The meeting over, we went to a nearby restaurant. William was frequently interrupted by greetings from friends and acquaintances, and by his own occasional excursions when he spotted a friend on the other side of the room. Everywhere he goes he is either greeting or being greeted. It's a hair-raising experience riding as his passenger, because he is liable to swivel round in his driving seat to call out a friendly 'Hello!' to passing acquaintances, in the middle of the most complicated traffic manoeuvres.

As we queued to pay the cashier, one of William's friends removed the bill from his hand and paid it. Apparently that sort of thing happens quite often.

'I think we should go to the office,' said William; I readily agreed. It had been a busy morning by any standards (except, apparently, those of the Rev William McCrea), and I was quite pleased at the prospect of a quieter afternoon. So we drove to Magherafelt, where the McCrea family home is, and where he is Chairman of the District Council, besides being the Minister of

Magherafelt Free Presbyterian Church. We sat in the Chairman's office while William commandeered the telephone and dealt with 'some things that have come up'. Obviously it wasn't going to be a quiet afternoon. One call among several was from a constituent who had been asking the authorities for weeks to mend the broken street lamp outside her home, because she was frightened that her elderly sick relative was going to have a serious accident sooner or later. Now, in desperation, she was approaching the Chairman of the Council after numerous delays by local officialdom. William made several phone calls and sorted the matter out there and then. Having exactly the same problem with my own parish authorities at the time, and contemplating several weeks of darkness past and, as likely as not, to come, I envied the people of Magherafelt their chairman. I discovered in the course of conversation that he deals with at least 10,000 cases a year – nearer 20,000 in some years – personally, and these come to his notice either through the Council or through the church. Many of his 'cases' bypass all normal channels and go direct to his home, which is always open to callers. Magherafelt is a 'mixed community' – which means that the population is roughly half-and-half Roman Catholic and Protestant. William asks no questions about anybody's religion before he helps them.

His Council business took about two hours, and he decided to leave other work unfinished and escape to the church so that we could talk about the book you now hold in your hands – the reason for my visit. We went to the impressive new building and sat in his study, which is strewn with books and records with the emphasis heavily on the books. William's congregation is growing fast, and is already a large one. He sees his pastoral responsibilities as the most important part of his life. 'I'm a minister,' he said, 'first and foremost.'

Later that afternoon we would be going to his home for tea, where I was to meet his wife Anne and their four children; and this by no means untypical day-in-the-life-of-William-McCrea was to end with him travelling eighty miles, the length of the Province, to Kilkeel, by the Mountains of Mourne. He was due to lead, and sing in, a 'praise meeting' at the Glenlochlan Orange Hall. It was to preach the gospel through song and also to raise funds for the purchase of Bibles, to aid missionary work in Kenya. His driver, Paul McLean, was due to arrive in the early evening. Paul drives William to his preaching and singing appointments, which often end so late that they get back to Magherafelt in the early hours of the morning. 'I hardly ever get to bed the same day that I got up!', William is fond of saying.

So we had only an hour or two to make a start. William pushed his chair back and looked thoughtfully at the ceiling.

'How do you want to do this?' he asked. I opened my notebook and switched on the tape recorder. How do you begin to describe a life which seems to contain more activities in a single day than most of us have to deal with in a week?

'Begin at the beginning,' I suggested. 'Tell me about your childhood. What was it like? When did you start singing? Did you always want to be a minister? How did it all start?'

William closed his eyes, thought for a moment, and began. At the beginning.

# 1: Childhood

If you take the Coagh-Stewartstown road out of Magherafelt, and drive south through the green rolling countryside of County Tyrone, you will come shortly to a minor road on your left, leading up the gentle hillside to a cluster of houses, and signposted 'Brigh'. If you then look in the other direction, towards Omagh, you will see in the distance a fine view of mountains. Those to the North are the Sperrins, beyond which is the city of Londonderry; and south from the Sperrins runs the range of hills and mountains which crosses the Province of Ulster from Londonderry in the North right down to the border in the South. And in the foreground, where the land slopes peacefully away before rising up in foothills and ranges, you will be looking at my father's farmland, and the home farm Ballywholan where I was born, the youngest of five children, in August 1948.

The past has a great value for me. I love to think back on my childhood days, not just because they were very happy, but because of the lessons I learned from my parents – lessons which I have valued, and benefited from, all my life since.

My childhood existence revolved round those two centres, Ballywholan and Brigh. Robert

Thomas McCrea my father, and Sarah Jane McCrea my mother, believed in hard work and strict upbringing, and that was what characterised my childhood. But I loved those days. I believe that in very many ways we were much happier than children today, even though we didn't have many of the advantages and entertainments that are available these days. It didn't seem to matter.

Life followed a regular pattern, largely because of the demands of the farm. When we came in from school, we would go straight upstairs and change out of our finery into farm clothes. Then we would have something to eat, and after that we went out onto the farm to help with the work. We worked hard – it wasn't just children's play, we had our jobs to do and they were necessary jobs, so we had to do them properly and well – and it was quite a while later that we returned to the farmhouse. And when we did, we had to do our homework. So there wasn't very much time left in the evening to do anything else. In addition, of course, each of us children – Whann, Ivy, Sharon, Anne and myself – had his or her particular household chores to perform, which had to be fitted into the day somehow.

People often say to me that it must have been a dreary and depressing way of spending our childhood, and that we must have been bored and unhappy. But we weren't! Of course we had no television, it didn't exist and if it had we would not have had time for it. Neither did we have music-centres or any of the modern ways of passing the time that we take for granted today. There were in existence various organisations we could have joined, like the Boy Scouts, but we weren't allowed to. Not for any reason of principle, but simply because there was so much to do on the farm. There simply wasn't time for us to go roaming the countryside.

Children today would perhaps feel exploited or victimised if their parents brought them up in such a way. And, if you just look at the sheer quantity of work that we did, it probably would seem a very hard childhood. But we were a farming family, and like all farming families of my acquaintance we took our way of life for granted. It seemed perfectly normal; indeed, it was the only way we could have managed.

Our childhood, however, was much more than farmwork, housework and homework. We were very close as a family, and we talked to each other. It's been said that conversation is the lost art that television killed. When people meet each other these days, or invite each other into their homes – it seems that they don't know how to talk to each other. They don't know what to say! They've lost the art of conversing with one another, in many homes; and instead, the television sits there in the corner blaring away, doing all the talking and taking all the attention.

We never went away for family holidays; farmers in our situation rarely do. The school holidays were times of much more freedom, and we enjoyed just being on the farm, helping in the hundred and one things that had to be done, and growing up in the fresh air and beauty of the countryside. But one very special summer my sister and I did have a short holiday; we went to my Uncle George and Aunt Lizzie's farm and helped them with their farmwork. They lived about four field-lengths away from us! I thought it was wonderful to be staying in a different house and helping them.

In fact I saw Uncle George and Aunt Lizzie every week, for each Sunday after church I went to their house and spent the afternoon with them. It was a real treat to me. I sat with my uncle and aunt, talking about what had happened during the week, and about what I had been doing at school since last I had seen them. They had no children of their own, and they took a real interest in all my activities. They gave me a tremendous affection and love which continues up to this very day – my uncle has since died, but my aunt looks on us as her own family. I'm glad to pay tribute to them for all they gave me during my childhood and afterwards. I remember that if it was raining, my uncle and aunt would come in their car and take us the two and a half miles from school – it was a token of their care for us which we really appreciated.

Yes, I enjoyed conversation. I enjoyed the evenings when, work finished for the day, we sat together as a family, before bedtime. Often my parents would allow themselves to be persuaded to tell us stories, and the stories we loved most to hear were the stories of our family; what our relatives had been like when young, and what those of our family now departed had been like. So we became close to our parents, and through the stories they told us, to our family circle.

I carry the name William McCrea, and it was given me because that was my grandfather's name. Everything I knew about him I learned from those family conversations, for he died before I was born. Indeed, all my grandparents had died by the time I was born. I never met any of them. I never had the privilege of sitting in a grandfather's arms, or of knowing the caring affection of a grandmother. There's an affection and love that is special to grandparents; I can see it when my children are with their grandparents. It's a joy, a light in their faces. I often say in my public meetings that if one has the privilege of knowing his grandparents, he has a rich blessing indeed. And the more I heard about my parents' parents, the more I wished I could have met them. (But, thank God, one day I will.)

Why would I have loved to have met them? It is a wish that has stayed with me into my adult life. Of course, part of that wish is a wish to have experienced and enjoyed the special love and tenderness that is uniquely a grandparent's to give. But the greatest part of it is a wish that I could thank them for what they have meant to me as a Christian.

For example, one of my most precious memories out of all the fireside stories is the story of how my grandmother (my mother's mother) died. My mother's parents were the late James

Alexander and Martha Matilda Whann, of Killywhoolaghan, Stewartstown. At an early age, Grandmother Whann died, and she had the sorrowful burden of leaving a very young family behind. As she lay near to death, those around her heard her singing softly and peacefully that beautiful old hymn, 'We have heard the joyful sound'. It was as if she had already laid her sufferings aside, and was being joined in her song by the angelic choirs themselves. Her weakness gave way to rapturous praise:

We have heard the joyful sound;
  Jesus saves!
Spread the gladness all around;
  Jesus saves!
Bear the news to every land,
Climb the steeps and cross the waves;
Onward! 'tis our Lord's command:
  Jesus saves!

Little did my grandmother know, radiantly singing those words so many years ago, that I would be given the tremendous privilege of doing just that – that her grandson would in reality be enabled by God's grace to spread the gladness of the gospel from the shores of Ulster, 'across the waves' to the farthest parts of the earth! Not by 'climbing the steeps', but through the ministry of song, for I have had letters from Africa, India, Australia, New Zealand and many other places where the records have been played and listened to. And because it has been my privilege to spread that gospel, of which my mother sang on her death-bed, the story of her passing is something which I shall always treasure.

A few years after Grandmother Whann died, one of her young daughters lay dying. And we were often told the story of how, as she grew progressively weaker, she became more peaceful. My grandfather and her brothers and sisters gathered round saw that she appeared to be looking at some beautiful vision, and in a strong voice she began to recite

> Gentle Jesus, meek and mild
> Look upon a little child;
> Pity my simplicity
> Suffer me –

but she broke off, and exclaimed, 'O, it's lovely! Goodnight . . . Goodnight . . .' So she died, and my mother often spoke of the wonderful reunion there must have been between the little child and her mother, and of that greater and far sweeter meeting between the two of them and the Lord Jesus Christ.

And then my father, not to be outdone, would come in with *his* memories, and tell us stories about his parents. He often remarked how similar I am in many ways to Grandfather McCrea, whose namesake I am. William McCrea was married to Annie McCrea, and they lived and farmed in that same farmhouse in which I was brought up. The same rooms and passages which I was familiar with had been their rooms and passages; they had seen the same views, walked the same fields, and each Sunday they had walked up the same lanes to Brigh Presbyterian Church, which we as a family still attended.

William McCrea and his wife Annie were hard-working, Godfearing people, but hard work and long hours never prevented them from faithfully rendering up to God all that was rightfully his. Each Sunday found the family at church. Grandfather McCrea was a senior elder, and a man of prayer with deeply-held convictions. He was obviously a formidable character. A local lady once stopped to chat with him, and remarked that the weather was very bad – a common enough observation in Northern Ireland! 'The Lord never sent *anything* bad!' retorted Grandfather very firmly, and marched sternly on.

God gave him a vision, that his son John was shortly to die, and that he himself would live exactly five years after that day. (These stories which featured death and dying were not considered morbid or unhealthy. The dying words of a loved one, especially a loved one that you have never met, are very precious to remember. We loved to hear them repeated.) The vision was fulfilled to the very day. Five years after my Uncle John died full of thanks and praise to God, Grandfather McCrea went out into the fields and urged my father to hurry up and get the crops in. 'Hurry,' he said – and these were his very words – 'for I can hear the Shepherd calling.' He died, praising God, that same evening.

Such stories have helped me in my Christian

life. As a child they thrilled me. We loved to hear about our grandparents. And I would so loved to have met them.

Music had its place in our family life, and we would often sing together. I loved the hymnbook, *Songs of Victory*. I began to sing in public before I was five years old, and my parents received many encouraging comments about my singing. At home, I had to buckle down to piano lessons, and these became part of my daily chores. I didn't enjoy practising any more than any small boy does! But I loved playing the piano. Once I was in the sitting room, where the piano was, and the door was shut behind me, I must confess that I used to get out *Songs of Victory* and have a grand time playing away at my favourite tunes. Until, that is, I heard my mother coming in and walking down the hallway; then I quickly switched to the practice that I was supposed to be working at. If that hymnbook had been my piano lesson-book, I would have gone off to my lessons much more willingly!

Two of my sisters also had piano lessons, but they didn't keep up the interest. I was the only one that was kept at it. I became known as a pianist, as well as a boy soprano, at an early age. At church, whenever the organist was absent, or during the school holidays, I played the organ at the church. It was a really beautiful pipe organ, and somebody had to go behind and work the bellows – a real old-time instrument.

When I was eleven years old, my parents were

approached regarding the possibility of me being sent to Westminster Abbey to train as a chorister – the invitation came through contacts which my music teacher had in London. My parents were favourably considering the idea – which would have meant that I would stay in London and be educated there, coming home to Ballywholan during the holidays. But I was enjoying life too much at home, and I said I didn't want to go. Instead, when I passed my eleven-plus, I entered Cookstown High School.

However, the decision not to go to London did not mean a curtailing of my musical interests – quite the reverse was the case.

Much of my musical activity was in the church, where I often sang at services. We attended church, Sunday by Sunday, as a family. We children attended Sunday School as well as the regular Sunday Services. I attended church for ten years without missing a single Sunday. I never resented it; it didn't occur to me to do so, even though on a Sunday we had all our usual farm duties and household chores which had to be done before we set off for church. I became a Christian at the age of eight-and-a-half, and I think I can say truthfully that I never rebelled against God or against going to his house.

On Sundays we got up at seven o'clock, and before we sat down to breakfast we had to do our farm tasks. We did no work over and above the absolute necessities – my father, as a good

Presbyterian, had been brought up not even to clean his shoes on a Sunday. Work was confined to 'works of necessity and mercy', but even so, we had put in a hard morning's work before we left for eleven o'clock Sunday School, from which we would go straight to the twelve o'clock morning service proper. The service started at that time because most of the congregation were in similar domestic situations to ourselves – it was a thinly-spread rural community of farmers, labourers, business-men and so on.

The church services were sober occasions, and everybody dressed up for them. And I still believe that's right, that people should take the opportunity of dressing properly and respectably to go to church. I'm saddened when I see the lack of reverence in many churchgoers today. Some girls enter church today dressed as if they were going into a place of worldly entertainment. How much more becoming it is, to see young ladies dressed modestly and femeninely. It is the house of God we come to, and we ought I believe to acknowledge this by the way we prepare ourselves for going there. (Though I wouldn't for one moment want anybody to stay away from church because he lacked fine clothes and expensive finery. And there's danger in the other extreme also: people can get so caught up and obsessed by formality and 'respectability' that in the end, that's all that there is to their worship! What really matters is being clothed in the righteousness of God, not the particular garments you happen to be wearing.)

I would like to single out one person from those early days at Brigh Presbyterian Church, a Sunday School teacher, to whom I am very grateful. Her name was then Miss Joan Watters (she's married now, but she was Miss Watters to us). She taught us faithfully and thoroughly, and I know that those of us who became Christians were her great encouragement.

Not that we were young angels! I remember once when Miss Roberts, another Sunday School teacher, was asking us questions about the Bible. And when she came to me, she asked me a question that I didn't know the answer to at all. With a sudden brainwave, I hit on the idea of pretending that I had lost my voice. 'Sorry!' I said in a dramatically faint whisper, sounding as though some fearsome infection had me in its grip, 'can't speak!' This immediately won Miss Roberts's sympathy, and she was very solicitous. 'Now, William,' she told me kindly, 'don't try to speak, because you'll strain your voice and that won't do at all. Just stay silent.' So I wiped the sweat from my brow and relaxed again.

Unfortunately, when a girl in the class a few moments later asked me surreptitiously whether I had prepared my school lessons for the next day, Miss Roberts's sharp ears overheard my gloomy but extremely healthy 'No I have not, indeed!' I can assure you that I got the best dressing-down I ever had from my Sunday School teacher, and I never once pretended ever again that I had lost my voice!

But I loved Sunday School, and in particular I

remember with affection and gratitude Miss Joan Watters, as she was, for the careful and systematic teaching she gave me in the gospel. From her I learned the truths which have meant so much to me, and many of us remember her with equal gratitude. It was a rich and happy part of my childhood, learning Sunday by Sunday about the things of God.

Indeed, my whole childhood was rich and happy. I thoroughly enjoyed it. People sometimes say to me that it must have been a very boring, uneventful childhood. It is true that the round of school, church and farm left comparatively little room for anything else. But we managed; and I look back and I am very grateful that I received the upbringing that I did. What we learn in childhood is what we draw upon in our adult life. In a real sense, I believe that what I was being taught then has been the underpinning for everything that I have done since.

It was strict upbringing, but that did not seem out of the ordinary to us. We took obedience and courtesy for granted, and we soon knew about it if we didn't. We had tremendous respect for our parents. We had to! And I would never have dared to call my father 'Da', either face-to-face or talking about him to other people. It was always 'Daddy'. And I assure you we would never have got away with calling him anything else.

Yes, I respected my parents. I still do. They're still alive, and I think they're the greatest people on earth.

## 2: A Christian Family

We were a strictly-brought-up, churchgoing, Godfearing family. My grandparents had died as Christians, and the stories of their Christian experience were part of our shared family conversations. And yet, for the first seven or eight years of my life, nobody in my family at Ballywholan was a real Christian. We were all unsaved. But when God convicted us, he didn't take long about it.

Before I tell how we became Christians, I should say what I mean by the words 'real Christian' and 'saved'.

The word 'Christian' often has little meaning today. Many people would call themselves 'Christians', but the lives that they live deny all that Christ taught – they say they are Christians, but they simply mean that they are not Buddhists, Hindus, Spiritualists or members of some other religious group. They think that because Britain is supposed to be a 'Christian country' (and how far from the truth that is today!), they are Christians automatically.

Others think that Christianity is the practice of good and decent living, not harming one's neighbours, showing goodwill to all people. My parents were decent, disciplined, hardworking members of the community, well-liked and respected by their neighbours and scrupulous in their church attendance. They assumed – and so did most people who knew them – that they were Christians because of the lives that they led.

But what our family had not yet discovered was that being a real Christian is not ultimately a matter of things that you *do*. It is a relationship that you enter into, between a holy God and a broken sinner, saved not by anything that he or she can do but only by the blood of Jesus Christ, shed on the cross at Calvary. The person who is saved by the blood of Jesus will find his heart changed, so that he wants to live a godly life; but without that initial surrender, no amount of godly living can save anybody. That is what I mean by the word 'Christian' and the Bible allows no other definition.

There is also much confusion today concerning the word 'saved'. 'I was shapen in iniquity, and in sin did my mother conceive me,' wrote the Psalmist (Psalm 51:5); and it is from sin that the Bible says we must be saved. What is sin? The best explanation I have come across is that by somebody who figures largely in my life and ministry – Dr Ian Paisley.

> The Shorter Catechism gives a tremendous definition of sin: 'Sin is any want of conformity unto, or transgression of, the law of God.' That is really just an explanation of the word used in the Greek New Testament which is translated 'sin'. It means, 'missing the mark'; failing to reach God's standards or, on the other hand,

going beyond God's boundaries into forbidden territory. (*Paisley: the man and his message*, 1976)

When God saves a sinner, he saves him, the Bible says, from the *power* of sin which has him in chains; from the *penalty* of sin which is death and eternal separation from God; and he gives the sinner also the glorious hope that in the future he will be saved from the very *presence* of sin, in eternity.

I have explained what these words mean to me because it is the reason for the change that came over my family when, one by one, we became Christians.

My brother's name was Whann – which was my mother's surname. He still farms at Ballywholan. He was the first of the family to be saved, at a meeting conducted by the late Edmund Sanford. Edmund Sanford and his wife were Christian Workers Union evangelists. They came to our local mission hall at Curglasson, about a quarter of a mile from our home. Whann went to one of their meetings; when he came home he had been converted. I remember well that he came home and told my mother. She was very taken aback by this announcement, but she was anxious to encourage Whann, and she said: 'Well, son, I'll help you the best that I can.' But she knew the truth in her heart. How could she help him? How could she, when she didn't have salvation herself? I believe that God used her own words that night to convict her.

And so my mother was next. The Rev Leonard Ravenhill, an American evangelist, was preaching in that same mission hall one night, and I was sitting by my mother's side as she realised that she needed to be saved. And within her a battle was raging, and she said to the Lord, 'Well, if somebody else raises their hand when the appeal is given tonight, I will as well.' (At the end of the meetings, the speaker usually invited those who wanted to become Christians to raise their hand as a public witness to that fact.) The Lord left her no escape! A little girl raised her hand at the end of the meeting, and so did my mother. She was saved that night. That was in 1956.

In 1957, my three sisters became Christians, on the same night. They went to a meeting together – I wasn't with them, so I don't recall very much of the detail of it, but at the end of the meeting there was an appeal, and my three sisters became Christians together.

Well, that only left my father and myself. And here I must again speak of my Sunday School teacher, Miss Joan Watters. I remember that whenever she spoke about heaven, it was lovely – I really enjoyed hearing about it, and she made it sound real and beautiful. But when she spoke about hell, it was a different matter. I was very afraid of hell.

Every night at home we prayed the Lord's Prayer. It was something we were taught to do, and every night, without fail, we got down and prayed. But later, when I was in my bed, I used to pray on my own account: 'Lord! Don't let me die tonight, because if I die I'll go to hell, and I don't want that' – because I was terrified of hell.

And the other thing that Miss Watters talked about, which also struck home to me, was the second coming of the Lord Jesus, when he would return and take for himself all the saved people, leaving behind those who had never repented and come to him. And so when I had finished praying that I wouldn't die that night I would add '. . . and, please Lord, don't come tonight!' And I remember that I shared a bedroom with Whann, and I used to wake up in the middle of the night and I would look across to his bed just to make sure that he was still there, because I was afraid that he would be taken when Jesus came back and I would be left for the judgement of God. I'd heard the verse about two people sleeping in the one bed, how one would be taken and the other left, and I was really afraid.

And then one evening Mr and Mrs Sanford were preaching again nearby, at a little place called Laghey, Dungannon. They were holding meetings there, and I went along, to hear Mr Sanford preach. And on the fourth of June 1957, I was saved at one of Mr Sanford's meetings.

And that only left my father – who by this time was possibly feeling a little threatened!

He never spoke against our new-found salvation. Even though his family had changed radically and a whole new dimension had entered their lives, and their conversation now would tend to leave him outside sometimes because he had not experienced the salvation that his wife and children had experienced, he never opposed or criticised.

He had been brought up as a strict church-goer, and he was indeed a committee member of the Brigh church; he never missed a Sunday. But he wasn't saved. He religiously observed his church duties. And he never, ever, got into bed without first kneeling and saying the Lord's Prayer. He used to drink; and I have known him, after an evening of drinking, still kneel at his bedside and pray the Lord's Prayer. Kneeling, not sitting. I don't know whether he ever prayed anything besides that, but he was faithful in his recitation of that prayer. And bringing up his family as a non-Christian, he gave us that God-fearing upbringing which I have already described. But he wasn't a Christian himself.

He became a Christian in May 1959, and I remember that night well. It was at the end of a gospel mission at Ballymaguire Old School, and again, Mr Sanford was taking the mission. And after the meeting my father went back to his car. And a niece of his went down to him – my cousin – and said to him simply, 'Uncle Bob; do you not think it is about time that you were saved?' And it was through that, after that young girl in her teens had talked to him about the Saviour, that he got out of the car, went back to speak with Mr Sanford, and got saved.

It's a sad thing to have to say, but our churchgoing wasn't altered very much by my mother and us children becoming Christians. Apart from the faithful teaching of Miss Watters and some like her, ours was not a church where the gospel was preached in its totality. We were never told that sinners had to have their sins washed away in the blood of Christ. So becoming a Christian in the full sense of being washed in that blood and being saved from our sins by the Lord Jesus Christ, didn't mean that we suddenly began to find the riches in our church life that we had previously been too blind to see. There weren't any riches there. And that is a very sad thing for me to have to say.

But when my father was saved, and all seven of us knew the salvation of Jesus Christ – that did make a difference! Our whole family life came alive in a new way, and our home was transformed. I can remember the seven of us, the whole family, getting on the tractor and riding into the fields very late at night – even into the early hours of the morning, sometimes – singing that lovely hymn,

When the trumpet of the Lord shall sound
  And time shall be no more . . .
And the roll is called up yonder –
  I'll be there!

This was something really great, something that our family could sing together. We were completed as a family.

I remember one other thing from those days. Just after I was saved, it was the lambing season, and I went into the fields with my mother. It was sunset. And I remember my mother and me sitting down on the grass, and the sheep and the lambs were running about, and we looked up into the heavens and we saw the sunset. And I can remember it well, as if it were only the other night – we never saw a sunset like it in our lives. It was like the most beautiful painting that anybody could ever have sketched. And I remember turning to my mother and saying, 'Mummy, if heaven is more beautiful than that – then heaven must be beautiful, indeed!'

And I think now of the words of the old hymn,

Heaven above is softer blue,
   Earth around is sweeter green;
Something lives in every hue
   Christless eyes have never seen.
Birds with softer song o'erflow,
   Flowers with deeper beauty shine;
Since I know as now I know,
   I am his, and he is mine.

And I saw it all with different eyes, because I saw it with the eyes of a child looking at the creation of my Father and my Saviour. It was a tremendous and a very happy memory for me.

I haven't talked very much about my schooldays in all this. The reason is that the centre of my life was my home and my church, and there was so much going on after school hours and in the holidays that school was just something that happened but to which I did not attach very much importance. In fact, believe it or not as you may, I can't remember very much about my school career at all! There was so much happening besides, that I got caught up in. But I remember that a newspaper article in 1972 said:

> Today he is well remembered by his classmates as he played a prominent part in the life of the school. Says one of them: 'Willie enjoyed nothing better than a good argument and was one of the most forceful speakers in our Debating Society. Although he expressed his views rather strongly he got on well with all of us.' (*Mid-Ulster Mail*, 11.11.72.)

As in 1972 I was doing a lot of speechmaking and campaigning for various causes, the reporter probably felt that he had unearthed a hint of things to come!

I passed, as I've said, the eleven-plus examination and went to Grammar School, and I took my General Certificate examinations which enabled me later to enter the Civil Service. I had no great ambitions to go to university. I suppose that passing examinations and gaining employment meant that I had a reasonable education and that I did reasonably well at it, but I think that I have learned a great deal more since. Experience has been the great educating influence upon me.

Through my schooldays I had a very strong feeling that God had his plan for my life. When I left at the age of seventeen, I still wasn't sure what it was to be. Perhaps I might have had a clue in the part I was given in one of the school plays. Each year we had a school play, which was performed first at the school for a limited audience of pupils and staff; then there were public performances to which the general public could come. In one of these plays, I took the stage in the character of a certain Dr Chasuble, DD, a minister of the church!

Be that as it may, the years of my childhood, like the years of anybody's childhood, were the foundations for what has happened and been done since. Whether you intend to build a one-storey building or a multi-storey building, you have got to make sure the foundations are properly laid. My parents understood that before they were Christians, and after they were saved, they gave us the priceless gift of a Christian family home. And I believe that foundations were laid for my life, not only in the work and love of my parents, but in the lives of their parents before them, whose example I have gained so much from over the years. There's a verse in the Bible that sums that up for me.

> We have heard with our ears, O God, our fathers have told us, what work thou didst in their days, in the times of old. (Psalm 44:1)

# 3: Setting a Course

All through my boyhood I showed signs of an interest in the ministry and in teaching people about the gospel. I became a Sunday School teacher, for example, at a very early age. And in the evenings – I think some people must have thought I was mad – when I was bringing the cows home, I used to preach the gospel to them! – although there weren't any converts . . .

There were a number of such things which all seemed to point to an interest and an aptitude in sharing my faith, and as I got closer and closer to my school-leaving, and as I studied the Word of God more and more and witnessed to others about the gospel, I became aware that this seemed to be God's direction for me. And so I began to think seriously about the possibility of entering the ministry.

There was no particular encouragement for this at school, and in fact I can't recall whether it was something I ever discussed with my teachers. I had of course told them about the gospel singing and testimonies which I was involved in, in mission halls up and down the country; but the call that I was experiencing was a vague one, and I wasn't ready to talk about it in terms of training and career while I was still at school. I just knew that God did have a plan for my life, and that he was drawing me deeper into his service, and that somewhere there would be a very particular job for me to do.

But one event that happened in my early teens was to have a lasting significance on my future career. There was a mission held near the very place where I had been converted, Laghey, Dungannon, and the speaker was a minister by the name of the Rev Ian Paisley. It was a tent mission, and it was the talk of the countryside, because many precious souls were being saved through the preaching of the gospel. And I remember that one night my father came home from the mission services and told us that while Dr Paisley had been preaching, the lights had suddenly failed and the tent had been plunged into darkness.

'What happened?' I asked curiously. 'Did he just have to stop preaching?'

'No,' said my father. 'He just preached on as if he didn't need any lights at all, and the meeting carried on without a break!'

'Did he not have any notes?' I demanded disbelievingly.

'Well,' said my father in admiration, 'I don't know whether he did or not – but I tell you one thing, he for sure didn't need them!'

We were all duly impressed at this prodigious feat of memory, or inspiration, and my father took us all along to hear Dr Paisley for ourselves. I remember that we couldn't get seats in the main tent, it was so crowded; they had had to unlace the side flaps of the enormous tent and raise them up so that people could sit outside the tent, down the sides, and though we couldn't see him very well at all, we heard him. The Word of God was truly preached that afternoon, and many, many souls were saved. It was a wonderful meeting.

When, after that, we used to hear controversy about Dr Paisley and later heard about his imprisonment in 1966, because of that afternoon when we had heard the gospel preached with power and conviction we found ourselves tending to take his side in the controversy. At that time, we had not met him personally – just heard him, as we sat by the open side of the mission tent at Laghey.

When Dr Paisley was imprisoned in 1966 for his part in staging a demonstration outside a meeting of the General Assembly of the Irish Presbyterian Church, protest meetings were held throughout the Province. One of these rallies was at Dungannon, where Mrs Paisley and some of Dr Paisley's fellow Free Presbyterian ministers were the speakers. I went along to the meeting, and afterwards spoke to one of the ministers and asked him a number of questions about the Free Presbyterian Church. What was its stand on the gospel? On doctrine? On the fundamentals of the faith?

And I also asked him what a young person who felt led to join that church – and was desirous of entering the Lord's service – could do, to find out more. He promised to send me some information, and in due course the promised material arrived.

The Free Presbyterian Church, I discovered, had been founded in 1951, on St Patrick's Day. It's first officers were the Session of Crossgar Free Presbyterian Church which had been formed of elders who had withdrawn from their churches when those churches had opposed a gospel mission which Dr Paisley was leading. The new movement grew rapidly in numbers, and its uncompromising stand against the Ecumenical Movement and liberal trends in the churches found widespread sympathy.

'The Free Presbyterian Church will have no fellowship with churches in the World Council of Churches, or those who have departed from the fundamental doctrines of the Word of God,' I read. The church had been named the Free Presbyterian Church because it would strive to be Presbyterian in doctrine but free from any association with apostate or liberal churches. As I studied the information that I had been sent, and thought the matter through, I became very interested indeed.

At this time I was still a Sunday School teacher at Brigh Presbyterian Church. There was a struggle going on in my heart at that time. A number of special events were being organised for young people in the locality, and at these meetings pop records were being played. These Youth Meetings, as they were called, were supported by members of the Sunday School staff, and at the end of some of them the minister or somebody would give a few words and maybe a prayer, and a few words of Scripture might be read.

I felt that there was a very real contradiction here. In these meetings, attended by many of our young people, the world's music and values were being heard. I felt that what I was teaching my class Sunday by Sunday was being undone by what was happening at the Youth Meetings in the week.

You see, I don't believe that there is any place for the music and entertainments of the world in the church. The church was never called into being to be an entertainment centre; it was brought into being to feed the flock of God and to spread the Good News of the gospel.

The Youth Meetings were just one aspect of the dissatisfaction I was increasingly feeling with the Irish Presbyterian Church. Another, and more fundamental issue, was the commitment that that church was making to the Ecumenical Movement – a commitment which gave me the deepest concern, because I was – and am – very much opposed to the Ecumenical Movement. And I was impressed by the fact that it was the Irish Presbyterian Church's involvement with the World Council of Churches – itself a confessedly ecumenical organisation – that had prompted Dr Paisley's march to the General Assembly, for which he was imprisoned in 1966, and had also been a primary reason for the establishing of the Free Presbyterian Church.

As I say, I was teaching in the Sunday School at

this time. But I was becoming more and more unhappy with the trends that I was observing in the church. The battle was a very real one. Should I continue to associate with the church, or should I make a clear-cut break?

For a long time, the one thing that kept me where I was was my Sunday School class. Many people urged me – Irish Presbyterians – 'Look, if you leave, you are leaving those children without the gospel.' Who knows, I was asked, whether the next teacher who teaches them might not be an unsaved person – just as I had been for a large part of my churchgoing and my parents had been for most of theirs – who neither knew nor cared about the gospel and the need of children for it? And this was my biggest battle. It was the trump card played by those who wanted me to stay.

But the Lord showed me very forcibly that I was thinking the wrong way about the problem. What, I suddenly thought, if I did continue in the church, and the Lord took me home suddenly? What would happen to the children then, if I should die? Was God completely dependent on me? Was it up to my choice to decide the spiritual fortunes of these children, or was God actually sovereign, as I believed him to be? As I studied the Word of God, I was clearly confronted with the biblical teaching on separation. I had to decide whether I was going to obey God's Word, or man's voice. God's Word says, 'To obey is better than to sacrifice' (1 Samuel 15:22), and this verse spoke to me very strongly at the time when people were urging me to stay in the church. And I was also challenged by the passage in 2 Corinthians 6:14–18: 'Come out from among them and be ye separate, saith the Lord . . . And I will receive you . . .' These readings deeply bothered me, and I had to pray and think the problem through.

And so the Lord brought me to that point, after much heart conflict and people urging me, 'Stay, stay!', where I was able to acknowledge that he was Lord of my life, and to bow before him. So I made my decision to leave, believing as I still do that the Ecumenical Movement is not of God. It is an organisation that unites those who affirm the fundamentals of the faith and those who deny them. And the Bible says that there can be no such union.

For some Sundays I just went to the Sunday School and left on my motor scooter directly afterwards, solving my problem by not going to the morning service. But this was only a temporary solution, and after a short time I made the break and joined Armagh Free Presbyterian Church. That was in 1967, the year before the Troubles started.

At this time, I clearly said: 'Lord, wherever you want me to be, please open that door. And wherever you don't want me to be, please close the door.'

In June of 1967 I left school. The employment situation was quite good, and I began to look for work.

I applied to the Civil Service because I needed a job, and at about the same time I made an application to join the Free Presbyterian Church ministry. When the reply came from the Free Presbyterian Church, it was in the shape of a letter from the Clerk of the Presbytery, asking me to go for an interview, on a certain date. I was quite happy about this, but at that time I hadn't told my parents! And then, a few days later, I had a letter from the Civil Service, also inviting me to attend for an interview. 'This is it, Lord!' I said. 'You're going to close one or other of these doors so that I will be able to know your will for me!'

The first interview that I attended was the one for the Civil Service. It was a straightforward interview, and I was accepted for a post in the Department of Social Services. I began work there, and I really enjoyed it. I was very happy indeed in that office, dealing with members of the public. I worked in the Benefits Office, so I began my working with people and their needs which has been the core of my work ever since. But over and above the element of practical training and experience in help and counselling, the job offered real satisfaction. I had a great time there.

At the interview, nobody had asked me whether I had any other job applications in progress, and I didn't think it was worth mentioning at that stage. However, when I began working at the Department of Social Security, I told my superiors that I had an application in to the Free Presbyterian ministry. They were quite discouraging. Their opinion was, that I should stay where I was because I had a far better future in the Civil Service than I could ever have in the Free Presbyterian ministry. They pointed out that examination results coupled with hard work would virtually guarantee me a rapid promotion.

Nevertheless, despite these encouragements from my superiors, and the fact that I was enjoying work in the Benefits Office more than I had ever imagined I would, when the day for my interview at the Free Presbyterian Church came, I was very excited.

It was a very daunting occasion indeed. The interviews were in the evening, but before the interview a more alarming trial was to take place. When the Clerk of Presbytery had sent me the letter advising me of the date of my interview, he had also sent me a verse of Scripture:

> Who gave himself for our sins, that he might deliver us from this present evil world, according to the will of God and our Father.
> (Galatians 1:4)

This wonderful verse was not exactly sent for my comfort and consolation. I was to preach a sermon upon it, immediately prior to my interview, before those who would be assessing my suitability for the ministry!

When I rose to deliver my sermon, I faced a congregation composed of Dr Paisley and all the ministers and elders of Presbytery. This rather overwhelming experience was made all the more so by the fact that I had never preached a sermon before.

Charles Haddon Spurgeon once told of a theological examiner who would sit in the front pew when one of his pupils was preaching in similar circumstances, and fix the poor student with a rigid and unbending gaze throughout the whole sermon, with predictable results on the student's peace of mind. I was treated very kindly, however. Dr Paisley is a very fatherly person. I think that in this respect he is little known. He is a man of great kindness, and he is very considerate to young preachers.

So it was that I preached the first sermon I ever preached in my life, at a few weeks' notice and upon a text which had been provided for me. I remember that shortly before I went in, feeling very awed about it all, the Lord provided me with this verse:

> Fear not: for I have redeemed thee, I have called thee by name; thou art mine. When thou passest through the waters, I will be with thee; and through the rivers, they shall not overflow thee: when thou walkest through the fire, thou shalt not be burned; neither shall the flame kindle upon thee. For I am the Lord thy God, the Holy One of Israel, thy Saviour.
> (Isaiah 43:1–3)

My first reaction to that was to think: what an odd verse to be given! 'When thou passest through the waters . . .' – it all seemed to be about trials and tribulations of very violent kinds. Well, I was certainly timorous that night, and the verse from Isaiah was a great comfort to me.

I preached the sermon. There wasn't much application that I felt willing or able to make to that particular august congregation, so I concentrated on giving what I hoped was a soundly biblical exposition of the meaning of the verse. Then when I had finished the sermon I was interviewed by the Presbytery, and after that I was sitting with the other applicants, waiting for the verdict. We had all preached our sermons and been interviewed, one after the other, so it must have been a demanding evening for the Presbytery, even more than for us applicants!

I was sitting with my friend Freddy, who was also going through the application procedure. I turned to him and said, 'How did you get on?' and he said, 'Oh, all right, I think.' And suddenly I felt a leap of certainty in my heart, and I said, 'Freddy, I have been accepted here tonight, and I know that the Lord has a work for me to do in the ministry.'

A short time later somebody came out and told us that we had all been accepted as students for the ministry. Between entering the Civil Service, and leaving to go into the ministry, eight weeks passed. They were happy and valuable weeks, but I was not sorry to leave. I was sure that the ministry was God's will for my life.

There was only a slight problem in my mind remaining. I had prayed for clear guidance, that one door would be opened and the other firmly closed. I had imagined that with two interviews, I would succeed in one and fail in the other, and so it would be quite clear what God's will was. But I had succeeded in both interviews! I was sure in my own mind and heart that God's will for me was that I was to go as a student to the Theological Hall, but I had not had that clear and unmistakable sign from the Lord that I had been looking for.

It came in a very astonishing way. My parents, as I have said, were unaware that I had applied for the Free Presbyterian Church ministry, so far as I knew. I came home the night I was accepted, and went to bed without telling them. I wondered when and how I was going to.

Then in the morning I got up as usual, and I went out to the farm to do some work or other. My mother was out there with me. Suddenly, without any warning, my mother said to me, 'William, I want to ask you a question.'

'Oh dear,' I thought. 'Here it comes now.'

'William,' she said, 'have you applied for the Free Presbyterian ministry?'

I do not know to this day how she knew that. I replied, 'Yes, I have. And I was accepted last night.'

Her reply was, 'Praise God! For that's an answer to prayer.'

There was God's seal again, I felt, as well as his word. And then I knew that I *had* to leave the Civil Service, for God had now unmistakably shown his will for my life. And I found it hard to understand why God should have allowed me to be interviewed by the Civil Service, accepted for a job, and actually to start work there; and then to be interviewed for the ministry and be accepted, and have to leave the Civil Service and start all over again. At that time it was hard to understand.

But now, looking back, I can see God's hand in it clearly. There in the Benefits Office I was introduced to people, I worked with people, interviewing them, dealing with their problems, for those eight weeks. And that has been a large part of my ministry ever since. The time in the Department of Social Security was not wasted. It was not a blind alley. It was part of the perfect plan of God.

# 4: Licensed to Preach

Life as a theological student, at the Theological Hall on the Ravenhill Road, was as busy in its different way as life had been on the farm at Ballywholan – and a great deal more uncertain!

Two days a week were spent at the Hall, attending lectures and seminars and discussions of various kinds, and the other three days were spent preparing sermons, doing work that had been set as homework by the lecturers, and writing papers for our teachers. It was a very full programme.

When we were received in as students, we were clearly promised, for our material needs – nothing. That was the basis on which students were accepted. There was no grant and no money was available from the Theological Hall itself, for me. And the Lord provided.

I had to live in Belfast, so I left the home farm and moved into digs near the Hall. The programme of studies left no time to take up part-time employment, and at the beginning I was completely dependent on gifts which came to me. The Lord's provision for me was a further confirmation of his guidance. But nevertheless, I can assure you that those were very hard days. We did not live in luxury! Many a time the end of the week came, and I literally prayed the money in, because I had no idea where it was going to come from. There was no source that I could readily see. And the Lord was good to me. As a student I needed quite a few books, which I had to buy for myself. The Lord provided the money for them. My father generously gave me a new car, and I had the upkeep of that to pay for; the Lord provided there as well.

I can remember many times when the money wasn't plentiful while I was studying. I came to Belfast from the country, but I got to know quite a few people; and many's the time they would say, while we were going around together, 'Why don't we just have a bite to eat?' And I'd make some excuse and say 'Sorry, I'm going up the town.' And the reason I was going up the town was that I hadn't got enough money to buy food. It was very good training! I don't think that to this day my father knows that it was like that sometimes – if he reads this, it will be the first time he's heard of it. But I felt that I couldn't live off my parents all the time. I had accepted the call of God, and I believed that I should rely upon God to support me. Though I won't deny, often I wept over it and felt very lonely.

The Theological Hall wasn't a grand building. It was just a room, first of all in the old Ravenhill Church, before the Martyrs Memorial Church was built; and then, when the new church was built, there was a house next to it called Ardenlee House, and the lectures were given in a room in the house. I was a student during both periods, having started in February 1968.

There were no luxuries; it was quite a spartan way of studying. And it's important to say that when one is going into the Lord's work, one isn't going into a cushy job – a missionary goes out to the farthest corners of the earth and more often than not he has to build his own church when he gets there. Many people have fanciful ideas about Christian service and Christian training, but I can assure you that when you actually start doing it, these fanciful ideas are removed!

We started at ten o'clock on our study days, and worked through until five with an hour for lunch. We had four main lecturers, on Tuesday and Thursday. We had the Rev Bert Cooke for homiletics; he lectured on the art of preaching. You had to stand in front of all your colleagues and preach, and after you'd finished preaching, everyone commented on the content of what you had said, the mannerisms that you had used, the mistakes that you had made, the things that ought to have been omitted, the things that ought not to have been omitted – it was a very humbling experience! If you had any pride in you, it got knocked out. This sort of criticism was something that Mr Cooke was an expert at, because he was so gracious. And there were lectures on the pastoral ministry, and on the art of preaching, and we put the theory to the test as I have described. And I can tell you that in the early days my attempts were anything but professional! (Though even today I wouldn't call my preaching 'professional', it's the wrong word. You can learn the rules and techniques, and there's a place for them; but while I think it's essential that you have the basics and that you don't go out into the pulpit as a greenhorn, there's no substitute for the nitty-gritty of experience. But you need the basic techniques, because you're going out there to glorify the Lord, to preach the gospel, and you want to do it properly.)

We also had the Rev John Douglas, who lectured on the English Bible, going through it book by book, teaching us the themes and purposes of each one. Dr Paisley taught church history, and the Rev Alan Cairnes lectured on doctrine and the doctrinal stand of the Free Presbyterian Church.

The doctrinal basis of the Free Presbyterian Church has much in common with the great doctrinal confessions of the past, and it is of course intended to be a summary of biblical teaching on the great fundamentals of the faith. These are:

1. *The Bible* We believe in the absolute authority of the Divine Word, and the verbal inspiration of the Old and New Testaments.

2. *Salvation* The church believes that the substitutionary death of the Lord Jesus Christ and his resurrection are the only means of salvation, through faith.

3. *The Holy Spirit* We teach that the Holy Spirit is a personality, not a force or a feeling; and that his work in regeneration and sanctification is absolutely necessary; as is his infilling of the believer who is indwelt by him, for power to witness and to live for Christ.

4. *The Trinity* There is but one living and true

God, and there are three Persons in the Godhead, equal in power and glory.

5. *Jesus Christ* We proclaim the eternal sonship, virgin birth, and Deity of our Lord Jesus Christ.

6. *His return* The church teaches the visible and personal return of our Lord Jesus Christ.

7. *Sacraments* We hold that besides the Word and prayer, God has appointed the sacraments of baptism and the Lord's supper.

8. *Baptism* Each member of the Free Presbyterian Church has total liberty to decide whether or not he should be baptised. The method of baptism is total immersion.

9. *The Lord's Supper* This has been appointed by the Lord, for remembrance of his death. The people who come around the Lord's Table are born-again believers. This sacrament is observed once in every month, by every congregation.

Many people feel that the Free Presbyterian Church is over-contentious, and that it spends too much time in public controversy. I would simply ask them to study the points outlined above. They are crucial to the biblical gospel. If looked at in isolation, each one would appear to be obviously essential to a fully biblical doctrine.

And yet, how many of them are being attacked today – not only by the unsaved who have always attacked them, those outside the church, but also by the unsaved *inside* the organisational church; often people of position and influence within the denominations, who publicly ridicule many of the things which the Bible plainly teaches! And if these things are important – if we believe the Bible and all that it teaches to be the revealed Word of God himself – it is vital that we defend them, that we do not allow them to be swept aside without protest. The Free Presbyterian Church was born out of protest. The founders of our church did not enter into controversy for its own sake. For many it meant the grief of parting from life-long friends and possibly relatives, to meet with a handful of people in churches that were despised and criticised.

They did it because doctrines were being eroded for which our Reformation forefathers died. Those very principles on which that great struggle was fought were being thrown away, and so Dr Paisley and others took the unpopular road because they believed it to be the biblical truth.

And so we studied these truths in the Theological Hall, and Rev Cairns showed us the importance and the meaning of the great Bible doctrines.

Shortly after I entered the ministry training, I was asked to become Dr Paisley's assistant minister. It wasn't a great academic honour – I was told, rather than invited; being assistant to Dr Paisley was a duty which was assigned to me, and other students were sent out to help from time to time at other churches. I was very happy to be Dr Paisley's assistant, and it was while I was his assistant that I first came into contact with Magherafelt.

My duties as assistant minister involved chiefly hospital visitation and taking the prayer meetings at the church if Dr Paisley wasn't there. Hospital visiting is still a large part of my ministry. I like to greet everybody in the ward – it means a lot to a patient if he is greeted by a visitor even if it's just a few words. Then as now, I would begin my time with the patient I had come to visit with a chat, maybe talking about things the patient raises; and then I would come to the main purpose, the reading of God's Word, followed by a word of exposition. Usually this would include a specific challenge. And I would have to remember that even though the curtains may be drawn around the bed, others were listening, and I would try to say something of general application. Then I would pray, as I do each time I visit nowadays, with the patient.

So in this area of hospital visiting I was gaining experience in the work which I was being trained for. Also on Sundays I might lead the service for Dr Paisley, introducing the hymns, maybe opening in prayer; or I might be out at another church preaching. At every service in which I was involved I was asked to sing. Gradually, my life's work was taking shape.

I had to stop working as Dr Paisley's assistant eventually because of illness. There was a sister congregation of the Ravenhill Church in Sandown Road, Belfast, which was nearby; and I was asked to go there and pastor that church for a period, still remaining as Dr Paisley's assistant.

But I became ill, and instead I had to go to Kilkeel for six months to convalesce, at the home of the Rev James McClelland. I was supposed to spend the time resting.

I remember very well the day that the Rev James McClelland came to Belfast. Dr Paisley had made the arrangements for me to go to his home, and he had come up to show me how to get there, as I had never been to Kilkeel. I parked my car near the Belfast City Hall, and he parked his nearby. He had a lunch engagement, and he asked if I would go as well, and then afterwards he would drive ahead of me and guide me down to Kilkeel. So, to enable a speedy departure, I had packed my car with everything that I possessed – all my clothes and some books and odds and ends. We had a really lovely meal. And then I went back to the car, and as I came up to it I noticed that the window was open slightly. When I looked inside the car it had been stripped bare of all my things.

I had cleared my digs; everything had been in the car. I went to the police, they dusted the car for fingerprints, but they held out little hope of success. And to this day I have never seen those things again. My clerical clothes – everything, had vanished. And I went to Kilkeel that day with just the clothes I was wearing and nothing else. They were all I had to my name.

I had little enough money, but when I got to Kilkeel I bought myself some absolute necessities. A woman from Belfast heard what had happened and sent me some clothes.

But Kilkeel was lovely. I spent a lot of time in a

Mr Stanley Cunningham's home, who treated me very well; and the Rev McClelland and his wife were more than kind to me.

So my theological training ended in some uncertainty, as I had not expected to spend six months doing nothing. But shortly after I left Kilkeel, I went to answer a call to a town some miles to the West of Belfast, on the far side of Loch Neagh.

Magherafelt.

# 5: Magherafelt

*Magherafelt Free Presbyterian Church*

I was Dr Paisley's assistant minister for a year, and I would like to place on record my respect for him as a minister of God's Word, and also my gratitude for the great kindness he always showed me during my training and which he has continued to show me ever since. As I conclude this brief account of my theological training, I would like to add a few words about him.

An internationally known figure, he is today the Moderator of the Free Presbyterian Church which he helped to found in 1951. He is also the Member of Parliament for North Antrim, and one of the three Northern Ireland Members of the European Parliament; and he is Minister of the Martyrs Memorial Church, the Ravenhill Road, Belfast, where the Theological Hall was.

As I have said before, the building that stands in Ravenhill Road is the 'new' Martyrs Memorial. The original church to which Dr Paisley came was a small church with a problem of declining membership. He quickly found out those people in the church who had a real burden for the gospel, and mobilised them; a series of evangelistic meetings which followed saw many people saved. The church grew to the point where the building was uncomfortably small for the congregation.

Dr Paisley's plans for a rebuilt church seemed preposterously ambitious to some of the church members. For example, he announced a target for one particular 'Day of Giving' of £1,000 in one day. Some committee members poured scorn on the idea. The figure was totally ridiculous! That amount could never be raised! The whole notion was not worth thinking about . . . But when the day came, God honoured the faith of his servants and provided £1,500.

The opening of the new church was a great occasion, at which I was privileged to be present and in which I sang and said a few words about the new church at Magherafelt, which I will be describing shortly. The Free Presbyterians are the fastest growing Protestant denomination in Ulster today, and messages read at the service included several from far wider fields – from new churches in America, Canada and Australia.

It was made clear at the opening that the Free Presbyterian Church is not a church that hates Roman Catholics. In his sermon, Dr Paisley said: 'There are a number of Roman Catholics who are with us tonight because they have specifically asked me if they could come. And I would say to you, friends, we are heartily delighted to have you with us! Amen!' And a spontaneous and rousing burst of applause welcomed the Roman Catholic visitors.

He has no love for the doctrines of Rome which

he rejects and to which he is totally opposed. He believes passionately that the Church of Rome has abused the Bible; but for individual Roman Catholics he has nothing but a deep love and a deep desire that they might come to know the Lord Jesus Christ as their Saviour.

Dr Paisley does not want to make everybody into a Free Presbyterian. He wants everybody to be saved, but that is not necessarily the same thing. He puts it wryly like this: 'I would never urge people to become Free Presbyterians – I urge them to be saved! We've got enough problems with some of the folk we do have! I preach the gospel, and if people get saved and then want to join the Free Presbyterian Church, that's fine.'

Like most public figures, knowledge of whom is so often filtered through to us by the media, he is, I believe, much misunderstood. He has been represented as a bigot and an ogre. In reality, he is a family man, a man whom children love (as my own will testify); a true pastor and a gentle and sympathetic teacher.

As I said in the last chapter, my official 'apprenticeship' to Dr Paisley ended with the attack of illness which sent me to Kilkeel. When I came back from Kilkeel, I went to Magherafelt, having been told by Presbytery while I was at Kilkeel that this was where I would be going. At this point I must fill in the background of my previous experiences at Magherafelt.

When I had been assistant at the Martyrs Memorial Church, and was also at Sandown Road

Church for that brief period before my illness, I had held a gospel campaign in Magherafelt. It was in July 1968, and there was great opposition to the meetings. Every door was closed to us. Repeated attempts to find premises met with flat refusals, and we eventually found ourselves with a piece of land, but nothing to put on it.

The campaign went forward, and God provided shelter for it. The story of how he did this demonstrates once again that if God is for something, then not only will no power on earth stop it but, very often, he chooses to use his miraculous power in the most extraordinary way.

We needed a tent for the campaign – something like a small marquee. I knew exactly what we wanted, because you could at that time get hold of army reject tents, which sold for about eighty-five pounds. Such a tent would be ideal for our needs, but I had no idea at all where I was going to find that sort of money – in 1968 it was a considerable sum to find. I mentioned it to my parents in the normal course of events, and continued to ponder ways in which the money might be found.

I didn't know it, but at home there was a cow that had gone down with milk fever – she lost the use of her legs after she had calved. She was lying down all the time, and her legs had begun to fester and bleed; my parents had had to partition off a section of the cowshed and sling ropes from the rafters so that the animal could be stood up every so often. This regular heaving of the cow onto its feet was intended to get the circulation going again and restore some use to the legs. It was a standard treatment, but in this case it just wasn't working at all.

One night, my mother was praying, and she said, 'Lord, if you bring this cow back to health, we will give whatever she fetches at market to your work.' And from that moment, the cow began to improve. She got onto her feet, and she was soon back in the fields.

One day she was out there, and was standing up near the road, just inside the hedge, and a car stopped with two men in it. They got out of their car, and looked intently at the cow. Then they drove to the farmhouse, looking for my father.

'Do you own that cow up there?' they demanded.

'I do,' said my father.

'We'll buy it,' said the men. And whatever purpose they had in mind for her, that cow must have been ideal, because they paid seventy-odd pounds for her. That, at that time, was the price of a healthy animal!

The money came to me, and I was able to buy my reject army tent, and that is the story of how the Magherafelt Free Presbyterian Church – for this was its very beginning – got the tent in which to hold its first gospel campaign.

From Magherafelt, I went on, after the campaign, to Scarva, near the border of County Armagh and County Down. We took the tent for our meetings there, and in Scarva, that tent was nearly wrecked. I arrived one night to find the seats turned over, the pulpit pushed aside, some of the main ropes slashed and all the side tie-ropes undone. The tent was just about to collapse. We found the culprits; most of them were teenagers. Apart from reporting the matter to their parents, we took no further action, and continued to preach the gospel in the tent; and souls were saved.

From Scarva we returned to Desertmartin, near Magherafelt, where our next campaign was to be. It was then that I collapsed and was sent to Kilkeel to convalesce.

So I returned from Kilkeel knowing that I was to be minister of a new church, and having had some experience of the local opposition that previous gospel outreach had aroused.

The work at Magherafelt began in November 1968. When I think of the opening of our new church ten years later in April 1978, it seems a very long way from those early days, when the tent was pitched in the town and the Rev Gordon Cooke, Minister of the Rashankin Free Presbyterian Church, took the new church under his care. When I arrived as the student minister on 6 June 1969, morning and afternoon Sunday Services had been established, as well as a mid-week meeting for newly born-again Christians. The nucleus of the church was, alas, tiny indeed. Only twelve people had been prepared to make the stand of becoming members, thereby declaring that they intended to separate from the churches that had joined the World Council of Churches. I used to call them the 'twelve apostles'!

When I came back, the church was meeting, not in the tent, but in a wooden hut that had been lent to the tiny fellowship by the Rev James Beggs – it had no windows, but the gaps between the floorboards provided an adequate supply of ventilation! We looked a comic sight to many people, as we picked our way through the gap in the hedge and made our way over to the insignificant wooden structure – 'The Magherafelt Free Presbyterian Church!' But there have been innumerable instances of great acts of God beginning in such humble ways, and we just trusted God to build us up as a church.

We were slowly beginning to find our feet and take stock, when a sudden and unexpected blow fell. The hut was needed urgently for another Christian work. We had had our grumbles about the wooden hut, but the prospect of having nothing at all to shelter us from the elements was a very sobering prospect.

I called an emergency meeting of our menfolk – there were about eight of us there. Their immediate reaction was one of shock and dismay, but by the end of the meeting we had reached a unanimous decision. We were assured of God's purpose to keep the testimony going. So we made plans to build a more permanent building. We felt ourselves to be in very much of a wilderness experience. But God encouraged us, and on 8 August 1969, Mrs William Lees, wife of the beloved brother who had sacrificially given us the land on which it was built, officially opened the Magherafelt Free Presbyterian Church Building, for the Preaching of the Gospel and in Defence of the Protestant Reformed Faith – a smallish, corrugated-zinc construction.

With this step forward, we began to see an increase in our numbers, and very soon it was essential to arrive early for services if one was to have any sort of a seat at all. So we made further plans; we would extend the building. We began this work on 20 September 1969, and finished a few months later.

Quite early in the history of the zinc building, it had been decided unanimously to change the afternoon service on a Sunday to an evening one. The reasons for doing this were several, but its practical effect was very noticeable. By having Sunday morning and Sunday evening services, we were providing a similar programme, and offering a direct challenge, to the local churches from which our members had separated themselves. Our stand was against the Ecumenical Movement; the issue on which I had joined the Free Presbyterians was the same issue that applied in Magherafelt. We saw a tremendous response to our stand on this, and once again we were faced with a problem of space. We met again to make our plans, and on 23 August 1970, Dr Paisley opened our newly expanded – width-wise – church. There was a wonderful feeling of anticipation and expectation at the meeting. Nobody who had been part of that small group in the earliest days of our church could have foreseen so rapid and so powerful an indication of God's hand on the work. Nor, I believe, could they have foreseen the future plans God had for the church. And that is something that is true of all churches; while struggling with small numbers and inadequate accommodation, it is all too easy to forget that what seems insignificant in the eyes of the world is a section of the mighty church of Christ, and God will honour the faithful preaching of his word.

Two factors made it impossible for things to go on exactly as they were. One was known, the other unknown. The first was the fact, accepted by many of the members, that the limit had now been reached. So far as extensions to the zinc building were concerned, we had gone as far as we could go.

And the other factor was one that none of us knew, though the possibility had crossed most people's minds. The devil was watching the rapid growth of the new church on Mullaghboy Hill, and he was planning a setback for us. The young church, just finding its feet and beginning to grow, was about to lose its student minister.

### *Dungiven*

On 13 June 1971, the Dungiven Orangemen had their outdoor service and parade.

To understand why this was such a significant event, you have to understand both what the Orange Institution stands for, and also what the annual service meant to the Dungiven Orange Lodge. The Orange Order is a Protestant organisation, affirming the Protestant way of life. It commemorates, on 12 July each year, the Battle of the Boyne, at which in 1690 William of Orange defeated James II and ensured the Protestant ascendancy. Much of William's support came from Ulster, and his name is honoured by Lodge members to this day. There is no official link between the Orange Order and the church, but there are of course many who belong to both, and 'the Orange' plays a very large part in the life of Ulster Protestantism.

My own association with the 'Loyal Orange Institution' goes back a long way through my family. My grandfather was for twenty years the Worshipful Master of Chambres LOL (Loyal Orange Lodge) 171. And after him, my father took over the Mastership and held it for over twenty years. So for well over forty years – nearly half a century – the Mastership of that Lodge was in our family. And since I was knee-high, I had a little orange sash; and every first of July, the band that headed our Lodge – the Stewartstown Amateur Flute Band – always marched the two miles from Stewartstown out to our farm. There would be other people there as well, and everybody would have tea, and we would all sit out on the lawn. And my father would always have a presentation or some other duty to perform; and then the band would march back again. It's a regular event that I can remember right from my earliest days. I have some reservations about the Orange Lodge; there are some aspects of it which give me concern; but it has always played a very large part in my life.

The Dungiven Lodge met in an Orange Hall

which had been opened by a past Prime Minister of Northern Ireland. The Ulster Premier had marched with the Lodge a previous year. The march had been an annual event for years and years. Each June the parade and the service were a public declaration of what the Orange Order stood for, and it had been accepted as such.

But that year was different. Protests were made by the IRA and by the Civil Rights movement. They wanted Dungiven to be declared, as it were, a 'no go area'. The demand was met by a radio broadcast by the Grand Master of the Orange Institution, the Rev Martin Smith, in which he called on all the Orangemen to attend. The broadcast defied a ban made by the Government of the day, for in response to the threats of those who promised to disrupt any march, the then Prime Minister of Ulster banned the marchers from carrying out their annual demonstration. I saw that ban as an act of appeasement towards those who had said they would come with sticks and stones to disrupt the event.

So the position adopted by the Dungiven Lodge was that a civil and religious liberty was being undermined – and these were two liberties dear to the heart of Ulster Protestants. They argued that to ban the march was a retrograde step, not a progressive one. It would deprive people of a liberty that had been enjoyed for many years. So it was that the decision was made and further affirmed by Grandmaster Martin Smith, that the march would take place as planned.

As a member of the Orange Order, and as a

fervent supporter of the Dungiven marchers in their stand for personal and civil liberty, I went along on the march too. And unfortunately I was arrested.

There were about half a dozen of us arrested that day. I don't think the choice was an entirely random one. In the government at that time there was a very strong anti-Free Church feeling, and anti-Paisley feeling was also running high. I was very much opposed to the government of the day. I believed that a policy of appeasement was being practised, and that the IRA were being dealt with far too weakly. All that was happening, in my estimation, was that the stand which would sooner or later have to be made against violence and threats was simply being postponed. I believe that the consequence has been a serious worsening of the situation in Northern Ireland. I've always thought that we in Ulster could learn something from the attitudes of the Israeli government towards terrorism. At any rate, I was an opponent of the government of the day – over that particular issue – when I marched out with the Orange Lodge of Dungiven.

I wasn't a Lodge Office-holder. I didn't even have anything to do with the organising of the march. My presence was simply for support and encouragement, and if I had not been there the situation would not have changed. In fact, I have only ever held a minor post in the Orange Order – a minor chaplaincy; because Free Presbyterian ministers are limited in the positions of authority that the rules of the Order allow them to hold.

This is how the arrest came about. An Orangeman had an army baton broken over his head, in the violence that began to break out early on. He was bleeding, and the baton was in two pieces. That was quite extraordinary, because it looked to me to be a good strong baton, and there it was in two pieces. I decided that it would make useful evidence later, and I kept my eye on it. I helped the wounded Orangeman up, and bent back down again to pick up the pieces of the baton. At that moment, everything went dark. My bowler hat had been jammed down over my eyes by a blow from another baton.

I must make it absolutely clear that I am in no way anti-Security Forces. I do not criticise them for carrying out the orders of the Government that afternoon, even though I happened to disagree very strongly with the Government's acceptance of Republican pressures to ban the Dungiven Orange Service. I'm not denying that we were roughly handled that day (the Press photographs of the incident would prove me wrong if I tried). But I'm not anti-police or anti-army, and I would not want to impede them in the work that they have to do.

Well, I was bundled into a police car and taken off to the temporary detention centre, which turned out to be an old hut out on the Limavady Road. I wasn't at that time a prisoner. I was just being held for questioning. At the centre, there were several officers. I sat down with one of them and he took down various details and asked me for identification.

Having supplied this information, I was sitting there when suddenly an officer arrived in great excitement.

'Come quick,' he said to his colleagues, 'and bring Reverend McCrea to see if he can cool the situation.' I was taken out of the centre, put back in to a police car, and driven to the scene of the incident.

There have been several published versions of what exactly happened, and I disagree with some of them. One version is that, having been warned not to provoke a confrontation with the Security Forces, the Dungiven Orangemen had stormed a police barricade and thrown stones at the police, thus turning a fairly stable if tense situation into one of pitched hand-to-hand street fighting. I would most definitely contradict that and say that the trouble flared up after the arrests were made. There was no stone-throwing until the arrestees had been taken away. But the action taken enraged them, and by the time I was brought back to the scene, real trouble had broken out. Apparently there had been stones thrown from the Republican side, and the resulting skirmishings had been met by police teargas canisters. The Orangemen were not prepared to give in easily. They had been challenged by the Grandmaster to 'march through a wall of steel', and this they were quite prepared to do.

It was certainly an atmosphere of resentment and tenseness. The Loyalists felt that they were making a stand for their liberties, and having come thus far would not turn back easily. I must say that I found it very strange to have been arrested – on a charge of riotous behaviour! – and then to be brought back to the scene of my alleged crime in order to quell a riot that had broken out in my absence!

It was felt that as a minister I ought to be able to calm the situation, and that I might have some way of controlling the marchers. I could not be expected to be answerable for the riot, because as I have said, I had nothing to do with the fact that the march had taken place, and was there as a supporter, not a high-ranking Lodge Officer.

And in the end, I didn't achieve very much in my role of peacemaker, because the first thing that met me on arrival was a teargas canister. And I can tell you, that was terrible. I've been told – and I believe it – that the CS gas used on that occasion was stronger than the gas that has been used in such situations since. I really thought I was going to die. I remember clearly that I lay on the side of the road, my mind half-stupefied by the effects of the gas, with all the commotion raging around me; and I was thinking, 'Surely, surely I have not come from a good home and a good congregation, to die along the road at Dungiven.' I can remember it distinctly; it was a chilling thought.

But I did not die on that occasion. Later that day, I was allowed to go home. As a result of that day's happenings I was to find my name in the newspapers, and later on I would find myself going to prison for what had taken place. But before that, a much more important event was due to take place in my life. I was going to be married.

At this point in my story I have to reverse direction and go back several months to introduce you to Anne Shirley McKnight. For she it was who was to become my wife.

When I was Dr Paisley's assistant minister, a large part of my time was taken up in travelling to preach at other churches and missions in the Province. That is how, you will remember, I had first come to Magherafelt. Among the churches to which I went regularly was Moneyslane Free Presbyterian Church, outside Rathfriland. As the visiting preacher, I met and was introduced to most of the congregation, and got to know some of them well. Among the young people at Moneyslane that I got to know in this way was an attractive young lady, the daughter of one of the managers of the Armagh-Down Creamery. She was a secretary at the Newry School of motoring.

There were not many girls in the various churches about whom I had such a comprehensive dossier, but Anne McKnight was different. I can't remember when we first realised that we had grown very fond of each other – neither can she! – but by meeting her at church services, and also at her home, I got to know her and found out more and more about her.

The life of an assistant minister studying at the Theological Hall was a very full one and it left little time for social activities; even less, courtship! But we managed to see quite a lot of each other by going together to gospel meetings where

I was preaching, walking together in the lovely Ulster countryside on the rare occasions time permitted us to do so, and meeting together at her parents' home, to which I was invited for lunch each Sunday that I preached at Moneyslane; I became very friendly with her family, and that affection has grown stronger now that they are my in-laws.

I proposed to Anne in due course, and she accepted. We were married in the Martyrs Memorial Church on 25 June 1971, twelve days after the Dungiven march.

We went to Scotland for our honeymoon with the matter of the arrest and the question of what action would be taken, still unresolved. While we were away, we heard that a summons was going to be served upon me for my part in what had happened at Dungiven. We accordingly came home a week earlier than we had intended, because we wanted to be in Magherafelt when it came.

We came back to 10 Highfield Road, Magherafelt. The church had purchased this property as a Manse for their minister, and the purchase had not gone through without considerable opposition and controversy in the local community. I am very glad to pay tribute at this point, however, to the fact that as the only Protestant family in a side of the street which is otherwise entirely Roman Catholic, we have always had the greatest kindness, friendliness and courtesy from our neighbours.

The Manse was largely empty when we moved in, and we began to make it our home, even though the summons had not yet arrived and the future was very clouded. On 1 July we came home from Scotland, and on Sunday 11 July we invited my parents to Sunday lunch at our new home. We were all gathered there after morning worship, and I disappeared upstairs. After I had been gone for some time, my mother began to wonder if something was wrong, and she came looking for me. I was groaning with pain and writhing on the bed. She called Anne, and together they got me into bed and called the doctor, who arrived, examined me, and dispatched me to the hospital without more ado.

When I went into hospital, the summons had not arrived, and in one sense we had cut short our honeymoon needlessly. However, it was a very good thing that we did come home early, because it meant that we were beginning to settle into our new home when I was taken ill. I was very glad of this. Anne's worries about the summons were now increased by worries about my health, and the extra security of having moved into the house ten days before was, I'm sure, helpful.

I spent the next day – the 12 July, the traditional Orange Day holiday, commemorating the famous Battle of the Boyne – in the operating theatre, having my appendix removed! And then in I think about ten days' time, I left the hospital. I found that the summons had arrived.

There were complications to my recovery – the wound wasn't healing at all well, so after a single day at home I found myself back in hospital to have the necessary post-operational treatment. So it came about that I went straight from my hospital bed to my trial, and from the trial back to the hospital.

The words of the Resident Magistrate at Limavady Court House are engraved on my memory to this day. 'I sentence you to six months in Her Majesty's prison, Crumlin Road Belfast.' It was in all the newspapers: Rev William McCrea had been given six months.

I lodged an immediate appeal against sentence, which meant that I could return to the hospital. I had sat through the trial with a tube draining the wound, and without an appeal lodged I would have had to go into the prison hospital or (which would have been the likeliest course of events) be sent back to the Mid-Ulster Hospital from which I had come, with prison officers guarding my bed. I understand that this would in fact have counted as part of my sentence, but I don't think I would have enjoyed having prison officers sitting by my hospital bed to make the trauma of hospital life even worse. So the appeal was a useful device to enable me to complete my treatment in relative peace; though later my Queen's Counsel advised me to drop the appeal altogether and accept the prison sentence. The fact that I was a known associate of Dr Paisley could conceivably, in that situation, have meant that the verdict of the Resident Magistrate at Limavady might not only have been upheld but increased! The advice I was given was that I should avoid drawing too much attention to myself at this stage by questioning the sentence.

At 10 o'clock on the evening of Sunday 22 August, I went home to the Manse bearing a heavy burden of anxiety and distress. I had just preached my farewell sermon to the church, and the next morning I intended to go to the local RUC barracks and give myself up.

The day dawned bright and sunny. I rang the police to tell them that I had formally dropped my appeal and was going down to the barracks. Having dropped my appeal, the full six-months sentence came immediately into effect. I said to the RUC that I intended to present myself at the barracks at half-past eleven that morning, and that if they could at all avoid coming to the house to collect me, I would prefer them not to do so. This they agreed to, and I rang our friend Ruth Badger and asked if she would drive me to the barracks. Then I said goodbye to Anne.

In the next chapter, I will be describing my time in prison. Before that I would like to say a little about our marriage.

It had certainly begun very oddly, and the strains that were put on Anne in those first months of our marriage were hard to bear. But she bore them. She is a remarkable woman, and it takes a remarkable woman to handle the sort of marriage that ours had become. As my responsibilities began to take different forms and the days began to get increasingly full, Anne demonstrated a flexibility and resourcefulness which made me appreciate my good fortune in having been provided by God with a wife who supports and helps me in every way. She is a very important part of the William McCrea story, and many of the things I describe would be impossible if I did not have her as my wife.

We didn't start our marriage in luxury. We had both been brought up in homes that were not poor – as I have said, my father was, in the goodness of God, a prosperous farmer – but we had not been brought up to expect that money would be freely available on demand. In our families we were not treated the way some children are today, being paid for things they do around the house and so on. We worked without expecting payment – my father never bought us off in that way. We just did what we were asked to do.

In my family, whenever one of the children got married, there was a gift from our parents, the same gift for each of us. The money was to help us to set up our home. But we were never encouraged to look for hand-outs. My uncle had a saying that became a family proverb: 'The softer you make your bed, the softer you lie on it.' I wouldn't say that my family was unusual in this, though then as now there were children we knew who had extraordinary quantities of money given them by their parents. Some children today have cash running out of their ears! But we were taught not to expect that, and we were taught that if we couldn't afford something, we could not have it.

It's the same in our marriage. We are bringing up our children – Faith (the youngest), Stephen, Ian and Sharon (the oldest) – in the same way, and for ourselves, Anne and myself have stood on our own two feet right from the start. It's a good principle. If you are always relying on financial help from your parents, you can't budget realistically. My parents' attitude to me was: 'Look, you have taken unto yourself a wife; and it's up to you to keep her.' And we're grateful to them for that.

Even in those early months, when I was in prison, we learned to live like that. In fact, the government helped us to carpet our house! It happened like this. Anne kept aside most of the money she received from the church, and lived on the bare minimum. All the rest of it she saved. The money was intended for carpets for the Manse. In prison, I knew that Anne was doing this, and I was determined that, come what may, I was going to do my bit as well. For work that prisoners do in prison, they are paid; and by the time I left I had advanced to the princely wage of thirty pence a week! I put my prison wages aside, because I reckoned that if I could save in prison, I could save anywhere. The other prisoners thought that I was crazy – they spent their money on cigarettes and small luxuries – but I stuck to it, and came out of prison five pounds the richer.

So we saved together, and when I came home we combined Anne's savings and my own, and we saved for a little longer, and we bought the carpets for the Manse with the money.

We've always believed in the value of saving, and we have never bought anything for the house on the hire-purchase system. And God has blessed us in this.

Our life was busy right from the start. When I was released, after serving only four months (I was released early), my recording career had not yet begun to play a part in my life, but I did a lot of preaching (and sang at the meeting where I preached). I conducted a great many missions up and down the Province, like those Mr and Mrs Sanford had led in my youth. We took a lot of open-air meetings, and I sang at these as well. It was through this continuous singing ministry that I was beginning to get some pressure from friends to make a record – but that will take a chapter of its own to describe!

In many ways, that part of our marriage was the easy time. It was busy, but not so busy as it is today, when so many demands on the time available have to be constantly juggled. My life these days is a series of appointments, and the diary is full for months ahead. I try to do things quickly, as they arise; if I put them aside to be dealt with later, they get buried under appointments and the next day's priorities. We were busy in those days. The work of the gospel allows nobody any time to sit back and be lazy. But life was certainly less complicated then!

# 6: Prison

On 23 August 1971, I got out of Ruth Badger's car at half past eleven, ready to give myself up to the police authorities. Standing there in the crisp morning sunshine, I was William McCrea, student minister of the Free Presbyterian Church in Magherafelt, newly-married man, and recovering, moreover, from a severe spell in hospital. By the end of the morning I was to be simply prisoner McCrea, 2474. My address for the next few months would no longer be 'The Manse, Highfield Road, Magherafelt'. It would be: 2474, cell 13/D1. My clothes would be, not my usual clerical wardrobe, but full prison regalia.

As a first-time prisoner (not counting an overnight detention previously on a similar case of conscience) I was technically a 'star' prisoner. However, 'star' treatment in the prison did not involve very much ceremony. I did have my photograph taken, but it was for the prison records; and I had to give all sorts of personal details and answer a list of questions. Then I was taken down to the basement, where prisoners spent their first night – I was there from my arrival until the next afternoon. When I was safely in the basement cell, the door slammed shut.

It was a terrible moment. The first really bad

moment when you go to prison is when you walk through the gates and you hear them clang shut behind you; but this was even worse. And the sound of rattling keys is something I will never forget. Big bunches of keys – you see them in television prison films, but the warders really do have them – rattle as the doors are locked. I stood in that basement room, and I felt totally, dreadfully lonely.

I had been allowed one privilege. I had asked if I could take my Bible in with me. It was a Thompson chain-reference Bible, which had been given to me by my father and mother. I believe that prisoners were usually only allowed the Gideon Bible which was provided in the cell. I don't know how rigorously the rule is applied, but I certainly counted it a privilege to be allowed the use of my own Bible, and I am grateful to those officials for it.

And I remember so well sitting full of emptiness and looking around that cell. I looked at the bars in the window. They were double bars – if you managed to break through one set, there was another beyond that! They were bars separating me from everything I cared for. They separated me from Anne, and I hadn't been married for very long. She had been in the Limavady Court when I was sentenced, and when the Magistrate announced his judgement she had collapsed in a dead faint. Now she was being cared for by our friends from the church; but knowing she was being looked after didn't make the walls any thinner between us. (Though I do want to say how grateful we were for the love and concern of those friends in the church, and our families, freely given at a time when we desperately needed help. Not all were so loving. I have to say with genuine sadness that during the whole period of my imprisonment, not a leading member of the Orange Lodge visited Anne at the Manse.)

And I was separated from my beloved congregation. As I sat in the cell, completely shattered by the quick and complete separation from Anne, I thought also of the service that had been held the previous night. It had been a terrible service, in that all one could hear was people weeping; though in every other way, it had been a wonderful service. How would they manage without a pastor, and how would they cope as a church with this strategy of the devil to stop our young church's growth? There would be some in Magherafelt who would be rejoicing to hear that I was in prison, I realised, and some would be hoping very much that it would mean that the Free Presbyterian Church in Magherafelt would be forced to close down.

So I was feeling extremely low. I just turned to God and I said, 'Well, God, you have got to help me. For if ever I needed reassurance, I need it now, and if ever I needed help and comfort, I need it now.'

My Bible was lying beside me. It was open, though not intentionally – it had fallen open at no place I'd chosen. I looked down at it, and the first words that I saw were those wonderful words of Paul in Romans 8:35–39:

> Who shall separate us from the love of Christ? Shall tribulation, or distress, or persecution, or famine, or nakedness, or peril, or sword? . . . Nay, in all these things we are more than conquerors through him that loved us. For I am persuaded, that neither death, nor life, nor angels, nor principalities, nor powers, nor things present, nor things to come, nor height, nor depth, nor any other creature, shall be able to separate us from the love of God, which is in Christ Jesus our Lord.

The assurance that I felt as I read these words, the sweetness of the Lord's presence, was unforgettable. I tell you, I could have reached out and touched him. He gave me the right word at the right time. You see, I had been dwelling on my separation from everything I held dear – friends, congregation, family, and, most of all, wife – and the Lord just said to me, 'Who shall separate us from *the love of God*?' It was a word right in season for me. I looked at the bars but I talked to the Lord. 'I'm separated from my loved ones – but, Lord, I'm so glad I'm not separated from you.' And I proved his love sufficient for me, in that prison cell.

It contained an old bed, and an oldfashioned dressing table, from which the mirror had been removed. It was getting dark and dismal, because the afternoon was nearly gone. But somehow the cell was more bearable now.

It came round to tea time. Suddenly there was an officer outside the door of the cell and the sound of keys. The door swung open and the officer stood aside to allow a prisoner to walk in, who was carrying an enormous can of tea – I think it was about five gallons. I stood up. I was given a cup – I'll never forget that plastic cup! It looked about a hundred years old, as though a million people had had the use of it before me. He also presented me with a rock bun. That was my evening meal, and very welcome it was.

The prisoner did not turn to go immediately he had given me my food and drink. He stood there and looked at me. He was a sturdy lad of average build. I found out later that he came from Rathcoole.

'You're the Reverend McCrea.' It was a statement rather than a question, delivered in a friendly Belfast accent. I nodded.

'That's right.'

'Don't worry,' the prisoner said. 'You're moving to my cell tomorrow, and you'll be working with me in the cookhouse. I've got it all arranged. See you!' And he went out.

That really came at the right time for me. It cheered me up considerably. The prisoner's name was Derek Jackson, and since his release he has become a born-again Christian. But that night he was just a friendly face, and I thanked God for him.

I had my tea, and I stretched out on the old prison bed and tried to rest for the night, awaiting the next day with trepidation and wondering how I was going to be able to last six months in this place.

And I was pondering things in my heart – the friendly prisoner, the knowledge of friends praying for me, and the passage I had been given from the Bible. At some time during the night, I fell asleep, but not before I had gone over and over the farewell service, the leavetaking at home, what Anne and my family and all sorts of acquaintances were doing and feeling at that time. And if I hadn't had that verse of Scripture, I don't think that I could have faced that first night, let alone the future. But I'll confess, I cried myself to sleep.

The next morning I was woken up by a bang on the door. I think it was about eight o'clock. You get different treatment on your first morning, when you're sleeping in that basement cell, to what you get when you've moved upstairs. And then I was allowed to shave – you had to collect a razor, because you weren't allowed to keep one permanently. I was given breakfast. And that morning I was taken to the Governor's office. He gave me a lecture on the do's and don't's of prison life, in a friendly enough way – he certainly didn't treat me as a minister! I was just another prisoner. But I wasn't expecting anything different.

I had next to go to the prison doctor for examination. The problem was that I still had a fresh wound from the operation, and it was not fully healed. The doctor immediately suggested that I should go to the prison hospital. I made an appeal to him not to send me there. I argued that I had been sent to prison, and I intended to serve my sentence in the normal way, and I didn't want anybody saying afterwards that I had been given a soft time in prison, or that I didn't know how prisoners really lived. I wanted to do my time like anybody else, and so I asked the prison doctor to allow me to go to the cookhouse as had been arranged.

After some time he gave in to this request and I was marched to the cookhouse (which was actually the prison kitchens, but everybody called them 'the cookhouse'). Before that, I brought my few prison clothes and my Bible up to cell 13, which is where I had been told I was to live for my time in prison. This was the cell also occupied by Derek Jackson. It was not an arduous removal operation. I had no belongings apart from the Bible and my prison clothes which had been issued to me, which consisted of old grey clothes – there was a nearly white T-shirt which went with them. For Sundays you had a brown prison suit – rather a glorified title for the unpressed jacket and trousers which had been worn by numerous prisoners already! With the Sunday suit a blue and white striped shirt was issued and a rope-like brown tie. That was my prison wardrobe.

Dressed in my working clothes, I went down to the cookhouse, and the first thing I had to do was scrub all the pans and big metal trays in which the food had been cooked. I stood for hours at the sink, scrubbing away with a steel pad. It was a horrible job. For a week or more, it was how I spent my time. A nasty old job, it was.

Upwards of thirty of us worked in the cookhouse. It wasn't a soft job – the 'soft jobs' in the prison were those outside the cookhouse! It was very tiring. But of course the pay made it easier. For eighty-four hours you were paid seventeen and a half new pence . . .

I got to know all the prisoners in the cookhouse and began to settle in. And then I was given a new duty – I was put on the 'baking line'. You went where you were told to go, and you did what you were told to do. Sometimes you were told to make the soup. That really was amazing soup. All the leftovers from the previous day – not the plate-scrapings, but anything left in the pans and the containers – was thrown in, any beans, any peas, any bits of meat, anything. Then it was all put through the mincer. As the day went on, any food that was left over or any extra quantity that had been made by mistake was put into the freezer to go into the next day's soup. There were some fanciful names given to that soup, I can tell you. I won't repeat them here . . .

Then, I remember, Derek Jackson and I got the job of preparing the potatoes. That was another miserable job. Some of the potatoes were soft and squashy, others were hard as nails. We worked away for hours, peeling and cutting, doing what we could with the bad ones, and I doubt if anyone fell sick from potato poisoning while I was in prison.

One thing that was particularly annoying for us in the cookhouse was the treatment given to the internees. Internment had just begun, and the prison was at that time housing a number of people who had been put there under the Government internment policy. They were treated as a different category of prisoner, and the practical effect of this was that we in the cook-house were like cooks in a restaurant, providing the internees with meals of a distinctly more luxurious type than we got. It was very frustrating to prepare special meals – real butter from Eire, Delft crockery, and a special soup – and then to see our own soup coming through that mixer! I will confess that I tended to do rather more sampling of the internees' food than was strictly necessary, but we had no scope for pilfering, had we wanted to – each pat of butter was separately accounted for, and you couldn't explain any absences away.

Internment was a bitterly controversial chapter of Ulster's history, but quite apart from its wider implications it was infuriating not only to serve special smoked fish to these prisoners, but to have to carefully garnish each portion with a sprig of parsley. After all, I thought with some annoyance, preparing the jug of mint sauce that added the final touch to the fish meal; this is the Crumlin Road Prison, not the Park Lane Hilton!

That is the kind of thing that occupied me during the working hours. In the rest of the week, I was occupied in a number of ways.

Each Sunday, services were held in the prison for the various denominations, and I lost no time in getting involved. The first Sunday, I went to the Free Presbyterian service, and Dr Paisley was the preacher. I opened the service in prayer, and I sang at some of the services while I was in Crumlin Road. It was one of the few things in prison that you really looked forward to, the Sunday service – that and the family visits. You never heard singing like it. The choir was outstanding. It was just great to hear those lads singing,

> Would you be free from the burden of sin?
> There's power in the blood, power in the
> blood . . .

And every night in D wing, the prisoners would shout out, 'William! Are you going to start?' And I had taken a hymn book into my cell (I'm not sure whether I was really supposed to) and I'd start singing. And I used to get that whole wing singing with me at the tops of their voices, the good old-fashioned songs of the gospel. We didn't get any bad reaction from the prison officers – short of stuffing our blankets in our mouths there wasn't really much that they could do to stop us! I think Paul and Silas would have enjoyed Crumlin Road.

That was tremendous. And also, every night, in the cell with Derek Jackson, I read the Bible and prayed afterwards with him. Then the lights would go out (they were switched off centrally from outside the cell), and I would get out of bed, kneel down, and have my own prayer time. Derek and myself had some tremendous gospel chats. I'm not saying that he gave me an easy time

– he asked some hard questions – but he was really searching.

Through the singing at nights, people began to find their way to my cell to talk to me about their problems. Some had problems at home with their families. Others were having problems in their marriages, and were worried about the effect that the prison sentence might have. Some were worried about public reaction to them in their communities, now that they had been to prison. They came along with the things that were troubling their hearts, and asked me for advice.

Besides counselling my fellow-prisoners, I helped them with correspondence, and often helped with petitions to the Governor for early release. I used to write the petition out for them, and they would copy it out in their own handwriting. Although it seemed very odd to be doing this when I was a prisoner myself, unable to secure my own release, it established a good relationship with the prisoners. We had some really wonderful conversations about the gospel, and I know of at least two people who became Christians during that time and are now still going on with the Lord.

Visiting was allowed once a week, and in addition I was allowed one extra visit a month from a church committee member, to discuss any needs and problems of the church and to keep me in touch with its general progress. I especially looked forward to Anne's visits. At all times, a prison officer stood in the room when a visit was taking place, listening to all that was said.

I never had a visit from my mother, and this was intentional. The thing that gave me most sorrow in my whole time at prison was her first letter to me. In it, she told me that the shock of my imprisonment had made her feel as though her world had come to an end, that her heart was breaking; and as I read the letter, and realised how much my mother was grieved by what had happened, it almost broke my heart. And I never would allow her to visit me in prison, and I don't think she could have borne it. We decided by mutual consent that she should not come. It was best that way.

I was very encouraged to get letters from outside. It was a great comfort to know that one wasn't forgotten, and I knew that there were those who were trying to secure my release. Early on I received the following letter:

> Here is the toothpaste and comb as promised. We also have enclosed some shaving cream and lotion and soap. You may find the paper handkerchiefs useful.

(I was grateful for the thought, but the note arrived without the articles mentioned – I imagine it was against regulations to receive gifts like that.) My Aunt Lizzie, who had been so kind to me as a child and to whom I was still very close, wrote:

> We are all thinking of you, we are counting the

> days and hours to when you will be with us again . .

A letter from the Rev James McClelland, minister of Londonderry Free Presbyterian Church, was also a great encouragement:

> As you will know, I conducted the services at your church and was very encouraged by the attendance at both services. I was particularly impressed by the numbers of people attending the prayer meeting before the evening service and the spirit of prayer which prevailed . . . Please be encouraged as you spend these months in the restricted confinement of the prison cell, and be assured that the prayers of many of the people of God are with you. Indeed, in our own church services in Londonderry there is never a prayer meeting held without mention being made of your name . . . God's people sympathise with you in your affliction and remember you in their prayers unceasingly. They pray that you may be strengthened, not only spiritually, but also physically.

And just before I was released, I had a letter signed by Mrs Wilson and Helen, two dear friends who visited me every week even though very often they were not allowed to see me, because of my visitor quota:

> We thank God that you are getting home. We are sure you are delighted yourself. I suppose this is the last newspaper we will be sending to

you here. We look forward (DV) to hearing you preach on Sunday night.

Truly, letters were a great strength and support. I have a bundle of 200 or more which I received in the short period of my imprisonment, and I treasure them.

Two more letters are of interest. The first is an example of the letters I used to write to the congregation at the church. I will just quote part of it.

> My dear Congregation,
>
> Yet again it is my privilege to write you these few simple words of encouragement and exhortation. I am turning to the book of Romans chapter 8; and therein we read these words: verse 31, 'What shall we then say to these things? If God be for us, who can be against us?'
>
> . . . [I then gave a short exposition of the text] . . . Wishing you all God's richest blessing, I close with the words of that beautiful hymn – 'Why should I ever grow weary? Why should I faint by the way? Has he not promised to give me, Strength for the toils of the day? Ever he walketh beside me, Brightly his sunshine appears, Spreading a beautiful rainbow Over the Valley of tears.'
>
> Praying for you always,
>
> Your loving pastor, William McCrea.

The letter was written on one side of a piece of prison notepaper (form 21/AD, initialled by the prison censor who had read it), and on the back is a letter to Anne. The two letters went together because it was Anne who read the church letter out to the assembled congregation at the service.

The second letter speaks for itself. It is addressed to Anne, is typed on a sheet of Ministry of Home Affairs notepaper, is signed by a departmental secretary and is dated 8 December 1971.

> Madam
> I am directed by the Minister of Home Affairs to refer to your previous correspondence addressed to His Excellency the Governor regarding your husband Rev William McCrea.
>
> I am now pleased to inform you that his case has again been considered and it has been decided to exercise the Royal Prerogative of Mercy to grant such remission as will effect his release on 9 December 1971.

What did I learn from my time in prison? I certainly learned something about facing extreme trouble and distress and also about adjusting to a completely different set of circumstances!

Looking back, I genuinely thank God for the experience. For I find it of great value. The Lord certainly proved himself to me at a time when the storms of life were raging more than any other time. Clouds had come over the sky, it was a dark day, and yet the Lord proved himself exactly what I needed. And when I needed him, he gave me the word at the exact time, not before and not after, but at the time of greatest need. And that word of God from Romans strengthened me not just that first night, but for the whole three-and-a-half to four months. It made prison bearable.

8

It has also been of great value in my counselling of others. There are many bright ideas around in counselling today. Lots of good advice is given, and formulae are recommended, books to read and so on. But the realities of life have to be faced, and it is essential that a counsellor should know something about them. It is not enough to say to somebody: Well, don't worry, the Lord will provide, be of good cheer. It's not enough, if you have not understood that person's need in reality. What prison has given me is an experience I can quote, so that, just as with sickness, I can say: Yes, I understand, and having felt as you do, I know what – Who – helped me. So it brings counselling down to earth, in the reality of afflictions and difficulty which you have tasted yourself.

There were of course some lighter episodes in prison, and I remember one of them in particular.

Various dignitaries visited the prison, and on one occasion a Senator – there used to be a Northern Ireland Senate – came and one of the prisoners he asked to interview was me. Unfortunately, I couldn't be found. And that was how it came about that I was reported Escaped from Prison, and a big hunt started all over Crumlin Road Prison.

What had happened was this. When we had finished preparing all the food for the prisoners, we would go back to the cookhouse after lunch and would usually sit and talk for a while together. But often, somebody might not be feeling very communicative – maybe he had had a letter from home, or a visit, or something like that, and he wasn't feeling very good company for a while. There were all sorts of odd corners around the kitchen which were ideal for this solitariness.

I had gone off for some such purpose, and I got back to find the whole prison turned upside down and everybody looking for me. I was quite taken aback to discover this! I had to report immediately to the Principal Prison Officer. And I can tell you I got the lecture of my life when I told him the truth of it.

I had been communing with myself in the potato store, and had fallen asleep on a pile of sacks.

The day of my release finally came. I had got into the habit of sometimes standing at a window on one of the top landings of D wing, from which you could just see Crumlin Road outside; and I had often watched children at play, women hurrying past with their shopping, even dogs wandering along. I had envied them their freedom.

Now that I was to be free again, those last few hours turned out to be the longest of all the ones I'd passed in prison. But it finally came to the time for me to go. I followed the normal routine of prisoners leaving and did all that was necessary. One of the prison Governors signed my Bible – he said he did it because I had been an 'exemplary prisoner', and had not disgraced the testimony which had brought me in there. I said my farewells to my fellow prisoners, many of them men whom I had come to know very well. I wished that I could have taken a good number of them out with me that day. I kept up my contacts with them – I go back to the prison and sometimes take the Sunday service there, even today.

I walked out of the prison doors to where Anne was waiting for me, with my friend Clark Scott. He drove us, not to the Manse, but to my Aunt Lizzie's house. I had had several requests for interviews from the Press, and there were hundreds of well-wishers. Though I was more than grateful for the kindness of my friends, I could not stand the thought of constant telephone calls and visitors, so I had decided not to go home for that first night but 'lie low'. I just wanted to be where I would not be expected to be. So Anne and I went to Aunt Lizzie's, and I had my first contact with a soft bed for a long time. For the first time in over three months, no doors clanged shut behind me when I got to bed. And there was no chamber-pot in the room to be emptied in the morning, in that dreary ritual which starts the prison day. I was free.

# 7: Magherafelt Again

I returned to Magherafelt on 10 December 1971. As many had told me while I was in prison, the devil's attempt to hinder the growth of our young church had failed dramatically; the impetus for the work had increased greatly, and the church was thriving.

My release from prison was marked by the decision of Presbytery to ordain me as a Minister of the Magherafelt Free Presbyterian Church of Ulster, for of course up to that point I had still been a student minister. On 28 January 1972 I accepted the call to be Minister of the Magherafelt Free Presbyterian Church, and so on 16 February I was duly ordained and installed.

We still had the fortunate problem of lack of space. As we had already known, our zinc building was not capable of further expansion. It was a good problem to have – much better than finding our church too big for our needs! But something needed to be done.

And so we began to look seriously at the whole matter of a permanent, purpose-built church building, one which would be our home and which would accommodate the extra numbers which we trusted the Lord to bring us in the days to come. We knew it would be a major undertaking as soon as we looked at the plans which were drawn up, but we were sure that God's will was for us to go ahead in faith, trusting him to provide the necessary resources.

On 9 June 1973, Dr Paisley officiated at the sod-cutting ceremony held on the site. It was attended by 1,000 people. It is, I suppose, possible to chart and evaluate the growth of the Free Presbyterian Church by the various sod-cutting ceremonies which Dr Paisley has performed! On this occasion he preached a powerful sermon, in which he impressed upon us that the main work of the church was teaching, and preaching Jesus Christ.

The laborious task of clearing the site was undertaken by men of the church, working voluntarily and in their spare time, under the supervision of one of our church members. This unpaid assistance from many of our congregation was vitally important to us. One of those labourers looking back has written, 'I can personally say that I got great satisfaction from helping to build God's house,' and that was something which everybody felt.

At this point in the story I must pick up another strand – the Magherafelt District Council.

From the time of my release from prison, I began to find an increasing number of people coming to me with their problems. Like any minister, I had already developed a pastoral ministry among my small congregation, but with the publicity surrounding my arrest and imprisonment, more and more people began to arrive at the house with a wide range of problems, and many of them were from outside the church.

This continued to the point where so many people were coming that, to make the best use of the time available, I decided to set aside each Thursday night as the night for an 'Advice Centre' – it simply meant that people still came to the house, but I tried to persuade them to come on Thursdays! The problems they brought ranged from the very practical to the intensely personal. In all cases I set my advice in the context of the gospel, not as a propaganda exercise, but because I believe that only the gospel offers a real solution to the basic problems of people, which cause all the lesser problems. In many ways this service was an extension of the ministry I had had in prison, when cell 13 on D wing had been dubbed 'the problem cell'.

Still more people came wanting help, and people began to urge me to consider standing for the local elections. That was the confusing and momentous time of local government reorganisation, and Magherafelt District Council was reshaped into a representative body for a very extensive constitutency covering a large section of Mid-Ulster. I stood for the 1973 elections, when five councillors were to be elected for each of the three council divisions.

I was a candidate, in the May 1973 elections, opposing some who had been in the Council for thirty years, and some who had been its chairman for long periods. We were operating 'proportional representation', and I certainly surprised myself most of all, and the other candidates, by topping the poll. I gained more 'first preference votes' than any other candidate.

The Council that was elected in those elections was almost evenly balanced between Republican and Loyalist members, with the Republicans holding the edge by a majority of one – it was eight of them and seven of us. In the elections for the Chairmanship, the Loyalist group put me up as their candidate, but of course we were outvoted by one vote, which was not unexpected! So I became Vice-Chairman, and held that post on the Council for four years.

When the elections to the Council were held in 1977, I again topped the poll, and this time another Loyalist colleague was elected. Thus when the nominations for the Chair were proposed, I was duly put forward, seconded, and elected as Chairman.

I would pay tribute to my Loyalist colleagues on the Council for their continued support and loyalty, having elected me Chairman now for the fourth successive year.

It is a very absorbing and interesting part of my life to deal with my constitutents. It's also gratifying to feel that you do have the confidence of those you were elected to serve. I make no distinctions between Roman Catholic and Protestant in my work, and both are welcome in my home if they need any help of any kind. And there are many opportunities to speak a word about the gospel, just as there were in prison.

I will not forget the time when, in the Chairman's room at the Council Offices, I led one of the Council staff to the Saviour. I had been conducting a gospel campaign in Kells and Connor, in County Antrim (which is where the famous '59 Revival broke out). A young lad, one of our Council staff, began to attend the services. We had a really tremendous campaign, and this young lad came under conviction of his sins.

One day he came into my room at the Council Offices, and with brokenness of heart and deep conviction he asked to speak to me. I had the joy of leading him to Christ and explaining to him the gospel. He was shortly to be married. Later that night, he came to the church with his girlfriend, and I had the privilege of leading her to the Saviour also.

If you include Council work, pastoral duties, and people just calling by at the house, it would be about right to say that I deal personally with at least 10,000 cases a year of people in some kind of need. In a busy year the figure can rise considerably higher.

But I was still Vice-Chairman of the Council on 23 August 1975, when we laid the foundation stones of our new building. Dr Paisley was unable to be present on that occasion, as he had been obliged to go to America for a funeral. We were privileged to have Mrs Eileen Paisley with us, who laid a foundation stone. I also laid one.

The building took shape slowly. At times its progress seemed dishearteningly slow, and I and the church committee had to take on the role of exhorters and encouragers of the congregation. But we assured them that the church would be opened on schedule, and that no corners were being cut – the materials being used were of the highest quality, and we did not intend to skimp just to save money and time. It was a definite policy in our building programme that only the best was good enough for God's house. After all, we do not scrimp and do things inefficiently when we build our own homes – so why should we think of doing so when we build God's house?

Finances played a large part in our thinking. We had a great deal of voluntary labour, as I have said, and I would pay special tribute to our builder, Mr Barclay Morrow, a church member and great strength to us over this time. He co-ordinated the work of the volunteers, which is a job which calls for patience and tact to get the best out of the available help. Also, we were extremely grateful for the gifts which we were given. Our gift-income designated for the church building, over the period of the project, was consistently high. I might add that we did, as is usual in major building projects, take out a bank loan to cover the very heavy capital expenditure; but such was the generosity of our friends and the goodness of God, that we cleared the debt in less than two years after the building was opened. This was a great surprise to many people, and a great joy to us!

A sad moment was the dismantling of the old zinc building, which disappeared to make way for the car park. The old building had held a great number of memories for us over the ten years – it had seen many souls saved, it had welcomed many of our new friends, and it had seen heart-aches, disappointments, and also encouragements. Through the cold winter nights, people had come to our services and sat in that hut and heard the gospel.

As an epitaph for our old zinc hut, this recollection of one of our church members will do very well:

> On the fourteenth of September 1969, I was invited by a friend to attend a Sunday night service at Magherafelt Free Presbyterian Church. I had heard much talk about this church but had never been before. I agreed to attend this service which was conducted by Dr Paisley's late mother. It was an experience I will never forget. I had never been in such a place before, it was just an old tin hall; and as they were putting on an extension, the roof was tied down with tarpaulin. As it was a very windy night this had to be held down with ropes. We had to sit on bales of straw, but it is a meeting I will never forget. I heard the gospel preached for the first time in my life. Mrs Paisley spoke on 'Hell', and the Lord really spoke to my heart that night. At the end of that service I knelt down at a bale of straw and asked the Lord Jesus Christ into my heart. Oh, it was just wonderful,

> I felt as if the burdens of the world had been lifted from my shoulders. I had Jesus in my heart and I was really rejoicing.
>
> ... From that night I was a regular attender. Many people laughed at us and said that we wouldn't be there long, but the Lord answered our prayers and the church began to grow in number as many people Sunday night after Sunday night accepted the Lord Jesus Christ as their own personal Saviour ... the Sunday School grew week by week as boys and girls from Magherafelt and the neighbouring towns came out to hear the gospel, the wonderful stories of Jesus ...

One more item from those last months in the life of the zinc hut is our Financial Report for 1977, in which I was able to say:

> Once again we present to you the Church Financial Report for the year, 1977. Very sincerely I thank you for your generosity as this report clearly shows. Indeed this has been an important year as it is the last year (DV) and Financial Report in this present Church building ...

The items of expenditure relating to concrete supplies, builder's charges, gallery railings and a host of others tell their own story of a building nearing completion.

The great day for opening the new building was 29 April 1978. It was a beautiful sunny day. The opening service was due to begin at 3 pm, but it became quite obvious early on, as people began to arrive, that the numbers of people coming was going to exceed all expectations. Arrangements had been made to have the proceedings relayed by closed-circuit television to a 2,000 seat tent, but as the time for the opening drew nearer it became clear that even this was not going to be adequate. It was thrilling to see the crowds coming up the hill, many of them with no hope of even getting into the tent. In the end we managed to fix up a public address system, and a large crowd were able to hear the service and enjoy the sunshine at the same time.

The service was a wonderful occasion. Dr Paisley was the guest of honour, and I led the opening ceremony and service. Many took part whose names have appeared already in this story. The keys were officially presented by Mr Barclay Morrow; Dr Paisley then declared the building open, and Rev Gordon Cooke led in prayer. That concluded the ceremony. The service began with my speech of welcome, and greetings were received from Presbytery and from representatives of Local Government. Dr Paisley preached. And a collection taken at the service, when added to the other gifts we had received that day, meant that a further £24,000 had been added to the building fund.

Afterwards, tea was served to 3,000 people, and many stayed on to the 'Great Evening of Gospel Praise' which was to follow at 7.30 pm. Rev Fred Greenfield was the chairman, Pastor David Cassell from Glasgow was the speaker, and items of music were contributed by myself and a number of guest singers.

It was a great day in the life of our church, and a great day in my life too.

# 8: Where we are today

In one way, although we have not come to the end of the book, we have come to the end of the story, or at least brought it up to the present day. I hope that the story of William McCrea has a good many more years to run in the Lord's service! But it is appropriate that the church and its building should have brought the story up to this point, because that is the centre of my life. I have described my work on the local Council; I have talked about my political sympathies and my other interests. I will be going on to talk about the records I have made and my career as a recording artist. But the most important thing in my life, and the thing that is the centre of everything, is the preaching of the gospel of the Lord Jesus Christ. I'm a minister first and foremost, and that is what I put first.

In this chapter, I want to attempt to give a picture of my life today, by selecting at random a number of elements which I think are representative of the kind of things I do. I hope that this will give some indication of the very real needs that people have in Ulster – as in any part of the world; and in sharing with you some of the things that I have been privileged to witness and be involved in, I hope that you will catch something of a vision of what God is doing for the furtherance of his kingdom in these days.

Let me begin where my heart is, and give you a picture of our church as it is today.

I wish that this was one of those books with pictures! Then I would be able to show you exactly what our new building looks like. It is a very beautiful building – our architect did a fine job. People come from far away to look at it. It's a brick building, with the main entrance at the end; the roof rises up into a broad gable, and a pillared porch which runs the width of the building has a roof which slopes down in an inverted arch which balances the gable. The whole effect is very impressive, and the practical value of having a wide covered porch area has been proved many times since.

Inside, we have a gallery to accommodate as large a congregation as possible, and the roof over the gallery and main congregation area is of cedar wood. The wall against which the pulpit stands is an expanse of brick, in which a text is displayed in bricks of a different type and colour from the rest of the wall: 'Woe is unto me if I preach not the gospel.'

I could go on for a long time talking about the many fine things in our new church, and the details which all combine to make it such a lovely place to worship God in.

But the important thing in any church is not the building, but the people of God who meet there, who are the real church. The building is just bricks and cement, but the people are the church of Jesus Christ on earth. So I will talk a little about the things that happen in the church.

On a Sunday, we have a Sunday School and a Bible Class, meeting before our main Sunday morning service which is at 12 noon – our district being a predominantly farming one such as I had known as a child. At 7 o'clock in the evening there is a prayer meeting which precedes our 'Old Time Gospel Service', at 8 o'clock. I usually sing at these meetings before I preach. During the week we have a women's prayer meeting, a men's prayer meeting, a children's meeting, a prayer meeting and Bible study, and a youth fellowship meeting. This last is held on a Saturday night, and a good number of young people come. In the summer, the Youth Fellowship does outdoor work, such as tract distribution. They also do a lot of community work – they visit old people and sing to them, they visit the hospital at Christmas for carol-singing, and they have organised outings for the congregation as a whole. Sometimes they visit other congregations and lead the fellowship meetings there.

The Sunday School has over 200 children, and these are divided up for teaching into five age ranges. There are over twenty teachers, and the teaching given is solidly biblical. We have a special prayer meeting each month for the Sunday School teachers.

We are not a church meeting on our own for our own sakes without concern for the community in which God has placed us. We place a great importance upon outreach and witness, and we encourage all our members to prayerfully consider their responsibilities in this matter. As a church, we have regular literature distribution, and we have many excellent opportunities to talk to people about the gospel as a result of this work. One experiment we have tried is the 'Gospel Line' – an open telephone line to my house, where, if anybody rang the number, I would sing a few verses of a hymn, read a Bible verse, explain it, and then answer any questions the caller might wish to ask. I would say the experiment was successful – if extremely tiring for the person who had to do the singing! For I did much of it all in person, 'live'.

Our outreach is supported by literature, which we feel to be a very important part of the gospel work, and much of the leaflets and tracts we use are designed and composed by our members.

For my next 'snapshot picture' of what God is doing in Ulster, I have to ask you to travel eighty miles from Magherafelt, almost to the border with Eire, to the town of Kilkeel. You will recall that this is where I was convalescing when I was told that I was to be sent to Magherafelt as student minister, and I am fond of the town.

In the region of Kilkeel is the Glenlochlan Orange Hall. It was there I was heading one night when I drove down the Newry Road, and by the time I got there the early autumn evening had turned to darkness. I was met by the organisers of the event I had come to lead. It was a 'praise meeting' – a type of gathering I frequently sing at. These services feature a number of solos, all of which are carefully chosen to present the gospel very clearly. The singer will usually say a few words about the songs before he or she sings them, and if there is a leader of the service he will also say a few words from time to time. As a result there is often no need for a formal sermon, and so the praise meeting can be a powerful attraction to many who would otherwise never dream of entering a church building to attend a conventional service.

The meeting at Glenlochlan had not been organised by one of the local churches, but by a couple of local Christians who had booked the Orange Hall for the occasion. The purpose of the meeting was, besides the preaching of the gospel, to help two Kenyan missionaries who were in need of Bibles for use in their work.

The hall was packed, and many of the people present were not Christians. I led a team of four singers, and sang solos of my own between presenting the other singers. They were local people apart from two who had travelled some way to be present; and they all presented the gospel in song and testimony very powerfully.

At the end of the service I sang my final solos, and gave a simple but direct appeal to the audience. I asked any who were wishing to accept the gospel, to come and see me and receive a booklet which I had with me (this is a simple biblical study of the first steps in the Christian life). Two did so. I had the joy of leading them to the Saviour and praying with them. I was able to ensure that they would be put in touch with Christian fellowship and a local church.

At one point in the service, a collection had been taken up for the missionaries. The sum of £217 was collected.

As I drove home from the praise meeting with my friend much later, we prayed together and gave thanks for the souls who had been saved. Driving through the City of Armagh, we noticed a group of soldiers and firemen at a building up one of the side streets. A bomb, we learned later, had exploded in a timber yard. We were sobered by this further evidence of man's sinful state, but we were praising God for his acts that night.

Let me take you, this time, to the City of Belfast, and the Queen's Bench. I was there to say some words in support of one of our local residents who had, two months earlier, been tried and found guilty of a serious criminal offence. He (I have changed some of the details for obvious reasons) had been sentenced to twelve months in prison. Unfortunately, his family situation was very bad, and since his imprisonment, his children had become very distressed. The trial judge had refused leave to appeal, and the case presently being heard was a plea for the right to appeal.

I spoke briefly of the man's previous good character, and the fact that his shame at what he had done had prevented him from contacting me when he was arrested, so that I had not been able to speak at the original trial. I pointed out that as his minister I did not wish to minimise the gravity of the crime, and that the prisoner had no wish to do so either. But if the appeal judge would permit him to appeal, then the prisoner would appeal for a reduction in sentence to allow him to spend Christmas with his family.

The appeal judge listened carefully, and then retired. When he returned, he gave his verdict, which came as a complete surprise to me and an even greater one to the prisoner.

Having regard to the evidence presented, he said, and to the prisoner's evident recognition of the seriousness of what he had done, he was going to change the sentence to a suspended one of two years. Consequently, the prisoner could walk out of the court room a free man.

There were scenes of great jubilation outside that court room, I can tell you. There were tears shed, and the looks on the face of the ex-prisoner and his sister as well were wonderful to see. I drove them to their home, and all the way, the man was marvelling that he had expected to be driving back to prison in a police van, with prison warders on each side.

I was able to preach the gospel to that man on that and on other occasions, and since then I have had the privilege of pointing him to Christ. I am grateful to God that he allows me to help in this way and by so doing, and in the preaching of the gospel to those who are helped, to breach some of the barriers and heal some of the wounds that exist in Ulster today, at a very personal, individual level.

I could take you even further afield – to Israel, where for the past two years I have taken a party of ninety people round that beautiful and historic land, which is similar in so many ways to Ulster. It has been a great joy to visit the very places where the Lord trod, and to see the same scenes that he saw and travel the same roads. While there, I was received at the City Hall of Jerusalem, where as a representative of Magherafelt Council I exchanged gifts with Local Government officials and had the opportunity for song and testimony.

Mention of the Jerusalem ceremony brings me to Magherafelt again, to our Council Offices, where I have my Chairman's room and where our Council Chamber is situated. I go there regularly, and I deal with Council business and also with the needs of constituents who have contacted me through the offices rather than at home. We have an open home – anybody can walk in; but sometimes people prefer to contact an office and leave a message, so there is usually something to be sorted out, and my desk more often than not has accumulated a number of urgent messages since I was last in. The Council business itself, of course, takes time – there are reports to read, minutes to digest, and so on.

As I have said, many of the people who come to me for advice or assistance never set foot in the Council Offices but come to my home. Often a farm labourer will come straight from his work to discuss some problem of his accommodation or something else that needs advice. The phone constantly rings, and Anne keeps notes of people who have telephoned while I am out. Callers at the house include constituents and also members of the church, who have their own needs and with whom I try to spend as much time as is needed. Our four children survive this constant coming and going with great tolerance, and the atmosphere in our home is a truly happy one. Besides all that is involved in the care of four children and coping with the irregular timetable that I work to, she has her own ministry of talking with people, and like most ministers' wives, she is very busy.

A great deal of my time is devoted to preaching. As in the early days of our marriage, I still speak at gospel campaigns, and one recent episode that comes to mind is the night of the great floods.

It really had been raining quite exceptionally. All day long the rain had just poured down, and down. I was sitting at home, waiting for Paul McLean who was going to take me to a mission down in Newry where I had been speaking each night for the previous ten days. The gospel mission was nearing its end; and, looking at the weather, I began to think that we might not get there that evening.

When Paul arrived, he said 'I just came into Magherafelt and the roads are flooded in some places. It's going to be a bad night.'

I got to my feet. 'Let's go,' I said. 'The longer we wait the worse it will get.' And soon we were out on the road, driving away from the house. We took the usual turning, down a steep road, and because of the driving rain we didn't see the water at the bottom. Before we knew it, we were stationary in the middle of an extensive patch of floodwater.

For one awful moment it seemed as if the car was going to float. The water was well above the bottom of the doors, and comparing notes afterwards we found that we had both shared the same fear – that we would have to open the doors to push the car, and be drenched from head to foot by the rush of water that would immediately enter the car.

'Put her in reverse,' I said to Paul, but he had already done so. For a tense moment nothing happened apart from the whirring of wheels in water; and then we heard the welcome sound of treads gripping road, and the car moved slowly backwards out of the flood. We saw several flooded patches of road on the way to the mission, but none were so bad as the one near our house. A film crew turned up there some time during the evening, and our local catastrophe was shown on the television news. But God over-ruled and watched over us, and we arrived at the mission safe and sound.

Mullaghglass Free Presbyterian Church was founded in 1971, and it is in the deep south of County Armagh near the village of Bessbrook. It was here that the mission was being held, and over the past week and a half we had seen God mightily at work, and a good number of people had been saved.

I mention the Mullaghglass mission because it

is typical of that part of my work which I believe to be the most important; the preaching of the gospel. Everything else is subordinated to that work. Although I see all the various activities which I am involved with as different ways of proclaiming and practising the gospel, the chief focus and centre of my ministry is the pulpit or platform.

So the Mullaghglass mission represents something very dear to my heart, and I would like to describe for you that evening service, to give you a picture of what happens at such a meeting.

We arrived to find the hall full, which was a very great encouragement, because we had driven a long way and had not known whether anybody would turn out on such a terrible night. We had prayed together in the car on the way down and God had wonderfully answered our prayer, because not only were we safely arrived at Mullaghglass but the hall was full.

The Rev Alec Chambers led me to the room at the back of the hall, and went onto the platform to announce that we had arrived. I came through after a few moments of preparation, and sang five songs. I accompanied myself on the accordion, which is a favourite instrument of mine; and as I generally do, I said a few words of introduction to each of the songs. I chose the songs the same way that I compile my records – seeking to gather together a number of different gospel messages which might speak to a variety of people present that night.

My sermon was on the text, 'It is appointed

unto man once to die, and after that the judgement.' I took as my starting point the Troubles, and spoke of the apparent injustice that there is in so many instances when violence is done and the guilty person appears to have escaped from any consequences. I try to establish a rapport with my congregation when I preach. It might be through humour; it might be through reference to shared experiences, as it was that night; or it might be by speaking very directly to the needs of human beings, as I have seen them often so sadly illustrated in my everyday duties.

And from that beginning, I preached to the congregation the gospel of Christ, the old-fashioned gospel of unchanging grace, and the precious blood of Jesus freely offered for us.

I always on such occasions give people the opportunity to respond to the gospel, by publicly expressing their decision to bow before a holy God in the grace he offers through the gospel of his son. So as we sang the last hymn I invited any who wished to be saved, to raise their hands.

Let me make it clear, this is not an invitation to 'enquirers'. If people wish to ask about Christianity, if they have any questions they want to discuss, then they can come to me at any time and I will be delighted to talk their problems through with them in the privacy of their home or mine. I would never say that a person who wants to have some questions answered has to make a public gesture. What the public gesture means is that a person has been convicted by God of his sin; that the preaching of the gospel has taken root in his heart, perhaps after having been heard over many years, and that now he wants to do something about it. He wants to say to God, 'Yes, I understand your offer of salvation through the undeserved sacrifice of your son. I understand that your day of grace does not last for ever, and I want to kneel before you and ask forgiveness of my sins.' Such a person is well past the stage of being an 'enquirer'. He means business with God, because God has convicted him of his sins. And so I believe that it is my solemn responsibility and privilege to offer that person the opportunity to take the step of faith there and then.

As all heads were bowed, five or six people raised their hands, some immediately, others, still grappling with the gospel challenge, after several verses of the hymn. I invited them to go to the front of the hall and into a room where counsellors were ready to talk to them. I always speak personally to people who have come forward, usually after they have been counselled and the counsellors have prayed with them.

The congregation dispersed, the newly born-again Christians went home (as at Kilkeel we have a booket which we give them, which contains some basic teaching about being a Christian, and we also ensure that proper follow-up is done and the convert is brought into the fellowship of a local church) and I rejoined Paul in the room at the back of the hall, where a tea was now laid out. One of the most pleasurable parts of a gospel meeting is the time afterwards, when the leaders of the church or the mission meet together and we talk over the way the meeting went, give thanks for those who were saved, and enjoy each other's Christian fellowship. At this particular mission I went back into the hall where a few of the congregation were still lingering together with some of the people who had been making arrangements during the service, and I sang more songs for about twenty-five minutes. Then, with the time nearing midnight, we got into the car and drove back to Magherafelt.

As we drove along, in weather that was still wet and dismal, we were stopped for a routine check by Security Forces. A very damp officer signalled the car and asked to see our papers. 'I've been preaching at the mission down in Newry,' I said, and he nodded and waved us on. These necessary hold-ups are disruptive, but it's pleasant when one is recognised by the Security Forces with a friendly greeting or a nod. As we neared home, I was again moved by the gospel's promise of peace in a country which has known such torment.

One aspect of my life which has not been mentioned in this chapter, or indeed in the book so far, very much, is my career as a recording artist. The reason for this is that because it has happened, for the most part, in London, it has not made a great deal of difference to my everyday life in Magherafelt and Ulster. Another reason is that for me, the recording studio is an extension of my ministry – but it is not the centre of my ministry. And so I have thought it right to first of all describe my family, my church and the community in which I live. But now it is time to describe how the records came about, and to do this we must once again retrace our steps in time.

# 9: A Recording Career

Looking back, I can't remember a time when I wasn't singing. Music, as this book has made clear already, has always been a major element in my life.

I remember the first time that I ever sang in public. It was when I was between the ages of four and five that I was placed on a little stool in the choirstalls of Brigh Presbyterian Church, to raise me up a little so that I could see over the top. It was the first of many occasions when I sang at church services and functions of various kinds.

Then, when I was around about eight years old, I sang at my first concert. I had been singing gospel songs up to that time, but this was a secular concert organised by some of the local residents. It took place near Stewartstown, so it wasn't far from home, and my parents, who normally didn't go to concerts and did not encourage us to go to them, allowed us to take part because we had been specially invited. With one of my sisters, I sang the song 'Two little orphans, a boy and a girl' – I was seated at my sister's feet, and no doubt there were some sentimental tears shed among the audience, for I'm sure we looked very sweet. The response from the audience that night was tremendous; we found ourselves local celebrities as a result, and invitations came for us to perform at other concerts.

It might have been the beginning of a career as a juvenile singer – I don't know. It never came to anything, because shortly afterwards, I was converted, and I just didn't want to sing at concerts any more.

But I kept up a keen interest in singing and of course I was still singing regularly at church. When later on I entered Grammar School, I joined the Donaghey Congregational youth fellowship, though I was still going to the services at Brigh Church. The Donaghey minister was a born-again Christian, with a great enthusiasm for the youth work. He allowed us to form a Christian Endeavour Choir, and we practised hard and were soon going around the countryside singing at gospel meetings where the Faith Mission was conducting campaigns. There were about thirty of us, and I was the conductor and also the choir's trainer. I was about sixteen at the time.

Then still later I entered the Free Presbyterian ministry, and that was also an opportunity to use my singing. There was a big meeting held every year at the Ulster Hall, and while a very new member of the Church, I sang at one of those meetings – the hymn was 'Victory in Jesus'.

And I've been singing ever since; I'm asked to sing at every meeting I take part in.

I have already mentioned that people often suggested to me that I should make a record. They would come up to me after the service and talk about the hymns I'd sung, and sooner or later the inevitable question would come: 'Have you ever thought about making a record?'

The answer to the question would certainly have been 'Yes!' I could well imagine that a record, sold in places that I could never hope to get to personally, and taken into people's homes to be played over and over again, would be a powerful extension, under God's hand, of the ministry of the gospel in song which he had given me. Making a record seemed a good idea. The question was, 'How?'

Today there are several records of Ulster gospel singers, and a thriving cassette industry as well. For example, the records produced by 'Let the Bible Speak' are on many bookstalls in halls where I hold meetings, and they sell very well. You will not easily find them outside Northern Ireland, but they are a valued side of the ministry of the gospel, and we have some good singers in Ulster.

But when I began looking for a way to make my first record, all that was in the future. There were few, if any, gospel recording studios in Northern Ireland at that time. The field I was entering was an uncharted one.

I discussed the matter with the members of the Martyrs Memorial Church, and eventually I enlisted the help of the expert who recorded the church services, and also of Ian McDowell, who was the organist. We finally arranged to have a record pressed by Pilgrim Records (my present recording company), but there was no financial commitment on their side – we simply hired the pressing facilities. The record would be issued on my own label, and I chose the name 'Calvary Trust'.

'Rev William McCrea sings his gospel favourites' was recorded in the Martyrs Memorial Church, with Ian McDowell as the only accompanying musician. We recorded it on the church's own equipment, and one great day in 1967 I held the finished product in my hands, fresh from the manufacturers.

That record was reissued in 1978 by Sharon, a division of Pilgrim, and it has the original cover and sleeve-material. For a home-made product it still sounds very well, and the church equipment did its job splendidly.

The sleeve notes were written by the Rev Frederick F. Greenfield, who was the youth who had sat next to me during that tense time of waiting for the result of our application for the ministry. It is very appropriate that the 'Freddy' to whom I had confided my sudden vision of God's call to the ministry that nerve-racking evening should write the sleeve notes for the album which was to launch my ministry in song!

In its first pressing the record sold about 3,000 copies, which was an encouragement to us.

For the second record, 'The King and I', we moved to London for the recording. Pilgrim still required me to commit myself financially to the recording, but this time we had the use of professional facilities.

Our recording team of Freddie Greenfield, Sidney Garvin, Ian McDowell and myself, crossed from Larne to Stranraer overnight, arriving early in the morning. We then drove to London, and arrived at St Paul's, Onslow Square – the recording venue – in the early afternoon. I can tell you, it was quite a ride! We were met by the producer, Frank Waller, who was very pleasant and helpful; which was fortunate, because I was very overawed by this new and rather overwhelming experience, and was extremely nervous!

But when I began to sing, and my friends were with me playing the accompaniment, my nervousness evaporated. I won't say I enjoyed it – my feeling when the session ended at seven o'clock was one of profound relief! But it was an exciting and stimulating experience. We recorded fourteen songs that afternoon, and, though we had been travelling all night, we did not bother to stop for a meal. I think we grabbed a sandwich when we could, but we were too intent on the job we were doing to do anything but press on.

A very pleasant memory is that when we were back home and the record was released, it was played at a meeting of the District Council. I was at that time Vice-Chairman, and the Chairman, who was politically my opponent, congratulated me on it on behalf of the council. Two items – 'Without him' and 'Remind me, dear Lord', were played.

'The King and I' has been a very successful record, and it did well from the start. So on the basis of two successful records, I was taken on officially by Pilgrim Records, and plans began for a third recording.

This marked a complete change of direction, because the next four records were all made at the ICC studios at Eastbourne. All the arrangements were made by Pilgrim. This time my journey was much easier – I flew to London direct and then took a train to Eastbourne. I was met by the producer again, but a different one.

'Hello,' he said, shaking hands, 'I'm John Pac.' And so I met John for the first time; since then he has produced all my records. He introduced me to Elisabeth and Helmut Hoffman, the directors of the studios, and they and everybody else were very kind. This time I was on my own, because instead of my colleagues from Ulster, session musicians were to be used. I found them to be extraordinarily skilful. Each song had to be sung several times to establish interpretation, harmonies and so on; and I had no music, because I don't have many of my songs written down. So the session musicians had quite a complicated task, but they did it with good humour and the end result – 'Because he lives' – certainly sounds very effective. I chose the songs myself, and the recording, which was much more relaxed than the previous one, was a very new, stimulating, and really very enjoyable experience.

One bonus was the town of Eastbourne itself, which I became very fond of. It really is a lovely place, and I was glad to have the opportunity of seeing a little of it after the sessions were over.

I now had three records behind me, and I was becoming well known as a singer who had made records. I even had some requests for autographs! There was a lot of interest also in the technical side of it – people were very curious about how the records were taped, what a studio was like, and so on.

At that time, my records were chiefly sold in Christian shops and church bookstalls. There was a fair amount of interest in the press, though not so much as there was to be later.

After 'Because he lives', the next record to be released was 'Worthy is the Lamb', followed in due course by 'Rev William McCrea sings for you at Christmas'. This record did well, because there aren't many records of good gospel carols. It has a photograph of Anne and myself on the cover with our children, taken in the Manse, which is an appropriate cover for a family Christmas record. Then 'Hymns old and new' was issued, which was something of a departure from the previous records. The selection of hymns is rather more widely-known than previously; we chose a collection of hymns which most people would have heard of, where maybe some of the songs on the earlier albums were unfamiliar to people who didn't know my ministry. It was the last record to be made at Eastbourne, and in fact only part of the recording took place there.

Looking back at my very happy time with the

ICC studios, I see it as the time when I really began to understand that the recording studio was now part of my ministry, just as the pulpit and church hall and tent were.

For 'One more valley', we moved very far afield for studios. I was approached by David Payne, the director of Pilgrim, and asked whether I would be prepared to consider going to Nashville in America to record my next album. His reasons were very simple. If we wanted to do our very best in this ministry, then we should look for the studios that were best equipped to deal with the type of music I sang. And the best in the world for this music were in Nashville. Would I like to try recording an album out there?

I had been abroad to Canada and America before, so it wasn't the great excitement it might have been. In fact I've never thought of Nashville as being very special, and I have little patience for the people who have sometimes said to me, 'How can you possibly associate yourself with all *that*?' – meaning the worldly entertainment industry. It's simply a place where a job can be done properly.

We flew to Nashville, and were booked into a very nice hotel just outside the town. The trip was paid for by Pilgrim, and Anne came with me, and I am very appreciative of the arrangements that were made.

The visit began disastrously, because I fell sick. Whether it was the journey, or the new environment, or old troubles playing up, or a combination of all those things, I don't know; but I began to think that I was going to have to cancel the trip and come home without ever seeing a microphone. It certainly dispelled any illusions of glamour I might have been harbouring, about being a Nashville recording artist! I was due to start recording on the Monday morning, and between our arrival on Friday evening and Monday's deadline, I simply sat in the hotel and saw nothing of Nashville.

And then on Monday, I just regained my strength. I woke up, felt better, and went to the studios. It was a miracle.

John Pac greeted me. He was producer, and there was a 'chart leader' who was in charge of the musicians. The staff at the Sound Stage Studios, where the recording took place, were exceptionally kind to me. I was a non-entity, but they treated me with every consideration. They tried to make me feel completely at home, and the warmth of their welcome is a very pleasant memory. A bond of friendship was established which we picked up when I went to record my last album to date, 'Born again'.

In between the two Nashville records, the compilation album 'The very very best of the Rev William McCrea' was issued. Of course I had nothing to do for this album, as it is just a collection of tracks from the earlier records.

This book is being written shortly after the release of 'Born again'. It was launched at the Ulster Hall, where I sang some of the songs to an audience drawn from a number of different places including representatives of Pilgrim records. One item in the programme gave me great pleasure. David Payne presented me with a gold disc to mark sales of 100,000 records. I had already received a silver disc, but this further confirmation of God's blessing on the ministry he has called me to in song was a very precious moment for me.

With the release of 'Born again', there has been a considerable interest in the secular press, and I am very encouraged by comments like these:

> Bert McCormick, manager of Symphola which distributes the record, said 'I've ordered 10,000 copies as an initial quantity – the same number we are bringing in of the new Police album. The new McCrea album is going to be very big' . . . It's a good album for fans of Country Gospel, and certainly an impressive performance.
> (*The Newsletter*, 17 October 1980)

> The Tyrone-born singer is poised to break into the American scene. He has already recorded two albums, including his latest production 'Born again', in Nashville, Tennessee, and the visits have produced invitations to give concerts. A distribution deal with an American record company is already on the cards. The man at the centre of the international interest remains surprisingly unmoved by the attention. 'Singing's an integral part of my ministry,' he said. 'Every record that's sold means another

home has been reached by the gospel message,' he added.

'I've had letters about the records and concerts from both sections of the community in Northern Ireland. I know that at a recent concert in the Guildhall in Londonderry there were many people from the Bogside in the audience.' (*Mid-Ulster Mail*, 16 October 1980)

I am grateful for the encouragement, but what gives me the most pleasure is that comments like these in the Press mean that my singing will reach more and more people, and the gospel will, as a result, be proclaimed.

For the recording studio is, as I discovered at Eastbourne, simply an extension of my ministry. I'm not interested in having a string of records to my name and all that goes with that. It means nothing to me. The response that I hope for from my records isn't sales (though I really did appreciate the silver disc in May 1979 and the gold disc in October 1980); it is that people should be convicted of sin by God, and brought savingly to himself. When I get letters from people who tell me that they have been born again through the records, it means more to me than any quantity of sales. And that's what it's all about. Homes I will never enter, places in this Province – in the world – that I have never been: they've been reached already because the records have sold so widely.

This means that the words of the recorded

songs are of vital importance. I believe that the music should assist in the presentation, but the words are the important thing. So they must be simple, easily understood, and contain a definite message.

I have been told that my style is 'unique', and it's true that I find it difficult to categorise my singing. I resent people who try to do so, because the truth is that I might sing the same song at two different places and sing it in two entirely different ways. One has to be open to the leading of the Spirit of God, and I do not allow myself to be bound by the straitjacket of a rigid formality.

When it comes to putting a record together, I'm compiling a selection of songs which will be received into many different homes. Different surroundings, different problems – so how does one compile a suitable selection which will benefit as many people as possible and speak to a wide range of people's needs?

As an example, take my most recent album, 'Born again'. In choosing the songs, I was trying to achieve a collection which would reach many different personal situations. 'Wasted years' is the first song. I remember singing it at the Ulster Hall. A woman of about seventy years heard it, and she looked back over her life, and saw it had been wasted. Another person came back to the Lord when she heard it, because she had been backsliding for many years, and the song brought her to that point where she desired to consecrate all her remaining years fully to Christ. 'The Christ who died for me' – that takes us to the cross, to the very heart of the gospel, and shows us where our deepest needs are met. 'We'll talk it over' speaks of a time in the future when we will understand the various paths that God has led us along. The song, 'At the river of Jordan', is a direct challenge to the unconverted sinner.

I have aimed to put together something which will speak to as many different needs as possible, and each song on the album is there for a reason. The fact that the reviewers have commented favourably on the selections from the point of view of artistic balance and changes of tempo is a pleasant confirmation of God's over-ruling in every area of the records, and it also says a great deal about the skills of John Pac. But what I see as the main purpose of the records lies in the area of gospel proclamation, and the real joy is to hear that they have been helpful to many in this way.

# 10: Troubles and Sorrows

Northern Ireland is known to the world for the 'Troubles', and nobody who has lived in Ulster for these past years can possibly have remained unaffected, in some way, by them. I think of young children and older people who have died by acts of violence, and though I might have no direct relationship or even acquaintance with the families involved, the shadow of their tragedy is cast over everyday life.

And yet it would be true to say that these things do not really come home to you until you have experienced them at close quarters. And I could certainly sympathise with the anguish and the suffering that the victims of the troubles were going through; but until I experienced that suffering for myself, I was limited in my understanding and consequently in the help I could offer. It is only those who have walked the same road who can help in the fullest sense.

As a family, we have shared in the sorrows of Ulster.

I remember that Saturday night in 1976 well; I had been singing in Hillsborough, at a praise service. And I finished with that little song, 'Tomorrow is in God's hands'. And before I sang it, I talked a little bit about the Troubles. How we lived in a land of tears, and how people lived in fear and uncertainty; for many of the congregation that night were fearful, some not even knowing what would be facing them when they got home. Many a person has returned home to find a gunman at the door; or has been sitting by the fireside when the knock has suddenly sounded that announces the arrival of the murderer. So there was fear in many people's hearts. And I was singing that tomorrow *is* in God's hands, and that in God's hands must be left all our plans and hopes.

I left the service and was driving home when I turned on the car radio. Somebody was talking about a bomb that had gone off earlier that evening in Cookstown, the place where I was educated – my childhood home was nearby. I found myself wondering who the victims were. Who had been involved? Did I know them? Instinctively I felt myself sympathising with whoever it was that had suddenly seen the evening turn into tragedy. Perhaps it was a family I knew well . . .

I suddenly thought, 'Perhaps the bomber is heading back to shelter in some Republican haven. He probably had his escape well planned.' I deliberately took the route through a known Republican area, hoping that I would see something out of the ordinary, some clue that I could pass on to the Security Forces to help them in their investigations. At a time like that, you want to help in some way.

I arrived home. My wife said to me as soon as I

came in, 'William, you've got to ring your brother.' And I telephoned Whann, and he broke the news to me. Two of my cousins had been victims of the incident. Whann said I should get down to the hospital as quickly as I could.

I will never forget the sight of my cousins' bodies for as long as I live. I will not. The only reason that I do not spell it out here and attempt to convey the utter horror of what had happened to them, is that some who will be reading this book are themselves the loved ones of those who died that night. And I do not want them to go through what I experienced, looking at the bodies of Robert and Shirley. A young lad of sixteen, a girl of twenty-one; both bearing the terrible marks of terrorist violence. The end result of what a bomb did to them.

They had left home that evening to visit an aunt's house – it was an ordinary social outing. They were driving along, not thinking about anything except the night's visit, when somebody stepped out from the roadside and waved the car to stop. They pulled to a halt. The person who had stopped them said that there was a car gone through the hedge; and had they got a flashlight? Because somebody might still be in the car, injured. So these young people had gone into the field to look at the car, in case somebody was injured – it was an errand of mercy. They didn't waste any time about it, either.

They looked in the car, but there was nobody inside. They began to look around the car, in case somebody was lying there having been thrown out of the vehicle. Then suddenly somebody shouted, 'Look out! It might be a bomb!' And because there was obviously nobody that needed help in the car, they all went back to the road in ones and twos, hurrying just in case.

Robert and Shirley were the last people to leave the car. People who were there said that it was is if they saw something in the field – they seemed to be looking at a point away in the distance. I don't know what that could have been. Whatever it was, it held their interest long enough for them to be still near the car when it blew up. And these two youngsters were cut to pieces.

Around the same time, my wife and I were going to a wedding at Enniskillen. As we drove through one of the villages on the way there, I stopped for petrol at a filling station. I noticed that the woman who served me looked very apprehensive. She was fearful in the way that many people have become over the years in this Province.

And I said to her, 'Tell me, dear; it seems to me that you're very worried about something.' And I had my clerical collar on; she said, 'Your Reverence, did you not hear what happened up the road last night?'

I replied, 'No, I did not.'

She said, 'Where are you going?'

'Down to Enniskillen,' I replied. She nodded.

'Well, then, you'll pass it,' she said.

Two landrovers full of UDR men had set out down that road last night, out for some purpose or other, laughing and joking – and not dreaming that on that road was hidden the weapon of death. As they went down the road, the second landrover set the concealed explosive off. At least two UDR men were blown to pieces.

And I remember that woman saying to me, 'You know, I have two lads in the UDR. They go out on duty and I never close an eye until those boys come home, maybe five, six, seven o'clock in the morning. I lie awake, and nobody knows how many tears I shed for fear my lads will not be coming home.' And she said to me, 'When they turn the doorknob I hear it, and I call them both by name. And when they answer, I just lift a silent prayer to heaven: "Lord, thank you, you've brought them home again."'

That's an awful way of existence. It's a dreadful way for a mother to be, lying awake through the night, always half-expecting tragedy to strike. And when she hears of a bomb exploding, always the instinctive thought: 'Is my boy involved?'

And as I drove on along the road, I passed the place where the tragedy had happened; and I saw the UDR lads' colleagues, methodically picking through the reeds, lifting up a few last shreds of flesh and placing them in plastic bags. And that was all that there was to be sent home to their loved ones.

That is the harsh reality of the tragedy of this country.

It strikes even closer. You leave behind the terrible wayside tragedies, the bombed shops, the child that walked into a landmine; and eventually you reach home. But for many hundreds of people in Ulster, their own homes have become the setting for acts of brutal violence. Everybody is a potential victim, and the dread of the terrorist throws a black shadow over the lives of thousands who will never in fact experience violence, but fear it always.

I remember very clearly the night that I came face to face with the Troubles, and I was standing in my own hallway at the time.

I was coming home with two of our elders, from a Presbytery meeting in Londonderry. We got back to the Manse at about two o'clock in the morning. While we had been at the meeting, Anne had been out visiting some friends.

As we drove up to the house, something unusual caught our attention. There had been a white frost that night, and up by the side of the house there were wheelmarks. Now, we have altered the house considerably since then, but at that time we never parked cars at the side, always at the front of the Manse. The elders who were with me said, 'You go into the house and put the lights on; and we'll go round the back and look around to see if there's a bomb or anything suspicious.'

So I went through the front door, into the hallway, and out to the kitchen, as it was then, to open up the back door. I asked the two elders, 'Is everything all right?'

'It seems to be,' they said cautiously. 'But we'll just have another look round, in case.'

By this time Anne had come in, and she came into the kitchen, closing behind her the door between kitchen and hallway. What we did not realise was that the front door was still open.

I called the elders in through the back door, and said, 'Well, we'll just have a cup of tea before you set off home.' And Anne put the kettle on to boil. So we were all together in the kitchen with back door and hall door shut, but the front door open . . .

The knock on the door came at about half past two. We were still in the kitchen. The knock came, not on the front door, but on the dividing door into the hall. It was a rough kind of a knock. The sort you have nightmares about.

I assumed, because I'd forgotten about the front door, that what had happened was that somebody had managed to get into the house while we were out and had been lying in wait, secure in the house itself while we were scouring the bushes in the garden. I was sure that this was it. The IRA had come to get me. This was finally it.

There followed one of those periods of time which seem to go on for hours but in fact are only a matter of seconds. In that interval between hearing the knock and actually doing anything, I took in the situation. The two elders were sitting at a table, which would be effectually concealed behind the door when it was opened. One of them was engaged to be married, and the other was the father of four children. I silently weighed the situation. There was no call for the elders to die on my behalf. The gunman had not come for them; he did not even know that they would be there. It was me that he had come for. Why should I allow them to be sacrificed for me? Why should they die because they happened to be drinking tea with William McCrea? And, I reasoned, how would I ever face it, if we were all shot, and I was the only one who survived? How could I have any peace, or be able to feel that I had done my best, if I lived on and the young man engaged to be married and the father of four children died in my place?

I looked at Anne. She was not going to die for me. The gunman had not come for her. Anne wasn't going to be shot, I decided. I wouldn't allow her to be.

So – and these things sound much more logical when written down in the cold light of day than they appeared to me in that fleeting, frozen pause after the knock on the hall door – I made my plan. The only thing I could do, if there was a gunman behind the door, was to walk straight for the gun. I would open the door so as to conceal Anne and the elders, and I would make straight for it. And he would probably pull the trigger. And then, when he realised he had got the man he came for, and that his job was done, he would run. He certainly wouldn't go looking for anybody else to shoot at.

I will always remember opening that door. Sure enough, there was a man behind it, and he held a gun pointed at my head. I put my plan into action and I walked straight at his gun, while his finger was on the trigger. But I thank God, I am still alive to tell the story. The man was the worse for drink, and he simply did not have the nerve to go through with what he had come to do. It would not be right to go into too much detail about what happened when the gunman appeared; but I can tell you that I went back into that kitchen giving thanks to God. For if that gunman had done the job he had come to do, there was nothing that I could have done. I was unarmed and defenceless.

Anybody who finds this incident something of an anti-climax has not understood the power of threat and violence over the lives of ordinary individuals. Though by God's grace I survived it, the incident took its toll of our family in distress and anguish.

It was not the only time that I have been faced by death. Had any of those attempts in the past succeeded, I would not be telling my story today. Therefore, I do believe in the sovereignty of God, and I do believe that until the day which the Lord has set upon my usefulness comes, he will watch over me and protect me, and keep his hand upon me. I rest upon the knowledge that 'All things work together for good, to them that love God' (Romans 8:28). One then carries on living as normal a life as one can.

It is certainly not easy. It has been hard for my family, for my wife, and my parents. Perhaps it has been harder for them than for me, because I lead a busy life and do not have much time to sit and worry.

Experiences like these help me when I am dealing with people. I can understand some of their fears, because I know the kind of situation that they dread. I never make any investigation of anybody's religious beliefs if they come for help; I do not ask whether they are Protestant or Roman Catholic. If their need is for help, then it is my duty and privilege to help.

I have had to counsel quite a number of people in the Troubles, and I think I have learned from my own experience things which are valuable. For example, I have learned that often, it is not so much important what you say, as when you say it. I remember a young lad in Belfast who was a tragic victim of violence – he was tortured and then shot. The IRA left his body to be discovered, and when it was found I received a telephone call from the family, asking me to go down and see them.

The family were totally grief-stricken – even more than one would have expected, because the circumstances were so terrible. And I remember the mother sitting by my side as the casket was brought into that home, bearing the earthly remains of a young man of twenty-one. And she looked me in the face and said: 'Please, Mr McCrea, pray that God will give me strength to bear this. For my heart is broken and I can't bear it myself.' That woman was on the verge of a nervous breakdown from the strain of the torture and the shooting. A scar has been left on that family, just as a scar has been left on my own, which the years will not remove.

And I remember that while I was there, the

clergyman from the local church came in. There were the five brothers in the room as well, and they were standing around the casket when the undertaker opened it, to let them see the body of the young man. The lid was off, and the family were overcome with grief; and the clergyman put his hand on one of the boys' shoulders and said, 'Now boys, make sure you don't let any malice enter your hearts, or thoughts of revenge.'

The boy turned round, tears running down his face. 'Your Reverence, if that's all you have to say to us, we don't want you here. That's my brother in that casket. Not yours.'

I felt for that minister. Much of what he said was good, and there would come a time when the family would need the lesson which he was trying to teach. There was nothing wrong in what he said. But his timing was wrong.

And I have learned over the years both from visiting the bereaved families of Ulster and also from my personal experience of tragedy, that there is indeed a time to speak and a time to keep silent; a time to speak and a time to listen. There is a language which is universal. The language of tears. And nowhere has this language been learned better than in Ulster. It is a language spoken by Protestant and Roman Catholic. The victim might be one or the other, but the whole community shares the grief. Old hatreds have not died, and the community lives in dread and sorrow.

What then is the answer?

I believe that there *is* an answer for Ulster, that

there is a road to take which offers peace and reconciliation. It is an answer of hope, not despair; of joy, not sorrow.

It is my hope for Ulster. It is what I work and pray for.

# Postscript: My hope for Ulster

I believe that anybody talking about the future of the Province of Ulster ought to begin by making the point that there are tremendous pressures, brought about by men of violence, to abandon the democratic system which historically we have lived by. And there are those in Ulster today and outside, who are actively working to overthrow our democracy and introduce a different system of government. And it's my belief that once you abandon traditional democratic processes and begin to walk that other road, then you are walking a road to tragedy. If there is ever to be stability in this country, then this is a matter which will have to be faced in these coming days. You cannot stand democracy on its head, and that is something which the politicians will have to accept if a solution is to be worked out.

For that reason I believe that a Christian should work to uphold the patterns and processes of the democratic system. You will have gathered as you have read this book that I have not always been a fervent admirer of the Government of the day, but my commitment to democracy is a commitment based on the conviction that therein lies Ulster's future, and anything which strengthens democracy therefore is for our advantage and good.

So political involvement, and working as an elected representative, have a real and valuable place in the struggle to bring security and prosperity back to Ulster. If I did not believe that, I would not have accepted the post of Chairman of Magherafelt District Council. I would not be a member of the numerous local government and other political committees which I attend. I would not have accepted the post of Vice-President of Local Government Authorities in Northern Ireland, if I did not believe in government and democracy. I am totally committed to them.

But, in the end, however valuable the political measures, and however much well-meaning reconciliation is done by individuals, there is only one answer, only one message that is going to save Ulster. And that is the old-fashioned message of saving grace.

Let me give you an example of what I mean. I remember a young man. He was a leading member of one of the paramilitary organisations, and he was very heavily committed to its aims. And before we condemn him, we should remember that many young people were – and are – feeling that legitimate government had failed completely to protect their lives and homes, and that the future of this Province which they loved – and I'll make no apology to any man, I love this Province too – was threatened, even that their very existence was threatened. And seeing only a prospect of death on every hand, and feeling that there were no effective measures being taken, they became disillusioned with the conventional forces of law and order.

Please understand, I am not condoning acts of violence. I do not condone those who put themselves above the law, but I can understand how these young people felt. To understand it, you must understand how completely abandoned these youngsters felt themselves to be. You know, there are people in this Province today who cannot sleep in their own homes because of the threat of violence. When night comes, they leave their homes and sleep elsewhere, because they do not know what may come out of the night. That's a terrible thing, to be driven out of your own home by a threat and a fear! And a growing young army of people felt that the only thing that they could do was to arm themselves against violence as their fathers had done before them. And that was what this young lad had done, and now he was deep in the middle of it all.

I was conducting a gospel campaign at the time, and he began to come to the meetings, simply because I was an elected representative and he wanted to hear me speak. He wasn't coming because I was preaching the gospel. He came along because he was interested in my work in the Council chamber. But he came along to the meetings, and he kept on coming, until one evening he expressed a desire for salvation and I had the joy of leading that young man to the Saviour.

Today, he is completely changed. He is training for the Lord's work, and he is preparing, God willing, to go out and preach the gospel of the Lord Jesus Christ.

But Ulster's troubles are not just those to do with the IRA and the struggle of Republican against Loyalist. Ulster's troubles are the troubles that all human beings have.

I can think for example of a drunkard, a man bound for years by the slavery of alcohol. I believe that alcohol is one of the great curses of our age, and it is people like him who make me think that. And he and people like him have heard the message of the Lord, that he will gloriously deliver all those that call on him, and they have been freed from their bondage. People say that they want nothing to do with Christ because they want to 'be their own master'. But who is the master of the person who nears a pub door, wants desperately to pass by without going in – and cannot do it? That person is under the mastery of alcohol, and it is a magnet that draws him in inexorably. But over the years I have known many alcoholics who have turned to the Lord for deliverance, and he has delivered them, and now they drink freely of the water of life. I think too of a brother who sings with me in many of the meetings, who used to be a pub singer. He will tell you, 'I used to sing the devil's songs in the pubs, but now I sing the Lord's songs for the gospel's sake.'

I think of people who have been demon-possessed. We are seeing a great rise of interest in the occult in these days, and all too often it begins with somebody playing with a ouija board. They get interested and soon they get caught up in it and it takes over; and before they know it they are enslaved by evil. But, thank God, in my ministry I have seen many people freed from that slavery, released by the power of God's love and cleansed by the precious blood of Christ. For there's one thing above all other things that the devil hates; and that's the blood of Christ. There is one thing that demons cry out against; the blood of the Lord Jesus, freely shed for us. You can talk to the demon about anything else, but claim the blood of Christ and you will hear the very shrieks. Only the blood of Christ cleanses us from all sin.

Another problem I see today in Ulster – and I believe it is a world-wide problem – is the soaring suicide rate. I have spoken to many, many people in the course of my daily work, who are on the verge of taking their own lives. I am saddened to see this rising tendency. Once people are so deep in sin and despair that they can see no way out, a voice comes to them, and it's the devil's voice.

'You know, you'd be far better to finish it . . . there's nothing worth living for . . . this is far better, to get away from everything, have done with it . . . you're completely tortured; the best thing to do is to be released from it.' And what he doesn't tell the poor Godless sufferers is that though they may put an end to the trials and sufferings of this life, they are going out into the trials and sufferings of eternity and a sinner's hell.

The troubles of the people of Ulster are not only

those to do with the terrorist, the bomber and the revolutionary. They are the common troubles of sinful, fallen man. The gunman or the terrorist, like the alcoholic, the demon-possessed, the suicidist and countless others, share a common and disastrous problem. They are lost, adrift without hope, in a world of sin, because they do not know God, and have not bowed before Jesus, the Saviour of souls.

And so I would suggest that the answer for all the troubles that beset my beloved Ulster – and not simply those to do with politics and violence – is a very simple one.

Christ is the answer.

He is an old-fashioned answer, but the problem is an old-fashioned one. It runs throughout history. Those four words sum up the answer to the problems of Ulster and the problems of the world. There is no personal problem, no national, no political problem, to which Jesus is not the answer. When I was in Israel, I visited the city of Jerusalem, and I was received at the City Hall. One of the senior Government officials, from the Tourist Department, was there. And I remember saying to him that I hoped that the freedom to preach the gospel would always be granted in Israel. I said to him,

'Sir, I am not ashamed of the gospel of Christ. Jesus Christ is not a threat to Israel; he is the answer.'

Jesus, who was wounded for our transgressions and shed his blood at Calvary, stands outside the door of sinners' hearts. He says in his Word,